The Intellect of the Mind, Body, and Spirit

How to Find the Path of
Least Resistance to
Optimal Health,
Inner to Outer Beauty,
and Inner Peace

Annahita Z. Van den Berghe, DPT

Copyright © 2021 Annahita Z. Van den Berghe

All rights reserved.

ISBN: 978-1-7367106-0-9

DEDICATION

To my children and yours, who naturally exude the innate brilliance we seek.

DISCLAIMER

Any readings here do not take the place of your doctors' or dietitians' recommendations and orders. There are diets and lifestyle choices that are highly beneficial to one individual but harmful to another. Therefore, this book is not intended to provide you with a personalized, professional service. Your current momentum may have taken you down a path where your survival and well-being is dependent on your current medical interventions, such as medications, specific diets, and health routines. If a more holistic approach is more appropriate for you, it may take time to develop it as you trouble-shoot with your healthcare team. If this information inspires you, present it to your doctor for approval before making any changes.

The author does not dispense medical advice or prescribe the use of any technique as a form of treatment for physical, emotional, or medical problems without the advice of a physician, either directly or indirectly. The intent of the author is only to offer information of a general nature. In the event you use any of the information in this book for yourself or anyone else, the author and the publisher assume no responsibility for your actions.

TABLE OF CONTENTS

DEDICATION iii

DISCLAIMER v

TABLE OF CONTENTS vii

INTRODUCTION 1

CHAPTER ONE 5
   Follow Your Inner Voice 5

CHAPTER TWO 13
   Musculoskeletal Well-Being 13

CHAPTER THREE 19
   Sports Performance 19

CHAPTER FOUR 25
   Combating Sedentary Lifestyles 25

CHAPTER FIVE 33
   Diet and Nourishment 33

CHAPTER SIX 41
   What Should You Eat? 41

CHAPTER SEVEN 53
   Pregnancy 53

CHAPTER EIGHT 59
   Weight Loss 59

CHAPTER NINE ... 81
The Mind and Body Connection ... 81

CHAPTER TEN ... 93
Mindfulness ... 93

CHAPTER ELEVEN ... 101
Abundance ... 101

CHAPTER TWELVE ... 117
We Are All One ... 117

CHAPTER THIRTEEN ... 135
Our Children ... 135

CHAPTER FOURTEEN ... 153
The Life Cycle ... 153

References ... 161

Acknowledgments ... 163

ABOUT THE AUTHOR ... 165

Foreword by Michael Khadavi, M.D.

In medical school, I remember wondering why a manual to life and wellbeing—a simple and evidence-based guide to living a happy and healthy life in a complex and confusing world—had yet to be written. Dr. Van den Berghe has done the world the great service of dedicating her life towards learning a diverse, 360-degree view of human health and well-being. Herein is her gift to us—summarizing this wisdom in easy-to-use ways.

Rooted in physical function, Dr. Van den Berghe's passion first impacted my life after an ankle surgery in 2015 when I became a patient in her physical therapy clinic. I quickly learned that something special was happening in her clinic, not only for me, but for all patients fortunate to connect with her. She blended manual therapies with exercise-based strengthening programs, modified activities, posture, and lifestyle, but also overflowed with positive energy, compassion, and a deeper connection with patients that helped everyone improve their various conditions. Since that time, I have sent many challenging patients to her, including my own family members, and have become familiar with the tears of joy from our shared patients when they tell me of the relief they accomplished within just a few visits with Dr. Van den Berghe that they had failed to achieve in the many months with other therapists. This so-called "magic" that occurs in Dr. Van den Berghe's clinic has stimulated a curiosity in me - how do her patients improve their pain and function so quickly, and what is it that she is doing to achieve such head-turning results?

After spending hundreds of hours with Dr. Van den Berghe as a colleague, friend, and patient, I have learned that there is no magic. Instead, Annahita brings a rare, comprehensive mindfulness of the complex and interconnected nature of the multiple systems of our mind and body, combined with pure compassion, to every patient she works with.

In her pursuit of maximizing physical function, Dr. Van den Berghe has taken the extra steps to achieve a profound understanding of inseparable fields of mental, social, and spiritual well-being. This deeper examination has yielded answers to some of the most mysterious questions: Why do we spend more time getting fit, more effort to find peace, and more money on healthcare while our happiness, waistlines, and relationships are not improving. How can we fly to the moon, easily access formerly incredulous technologies, and effortlessly communicate with humans anywhere on the planet yet struggle to achieve the meaningful connections we require and find the balance and well-being we *struggle* to even imagine? Basically, how are we doing more and accomplishing less?

Over the years I have pushed Dr. Van den Berghe to share her unique knowledge with the rest of our medical and non-medical communities. I am proud and ecstatic that she has dedicated herself to writing and passing on her knowledge of physical, mental, social, and spiritual health to the rest of our world.

Enjoy!

Michael Khadavi, M.D.
Kansas City Orthopedic Alliance
Physical Medicine and Rehabilitation
Sports Medicine, CAQ
Team Physician: Kansas City Ballet and Sporting Kansas City

Foreword by Dr. Gary Gray

"Everything is connected" is the seamless message of *The Intellect of the Mind, Body, and Spirit*. With the use of capturing stories and resonating quotes, Anna van den Berghe shares with us her experience and wisdom that allows us to "bulletproof our lives."

A term I use to describe the interdependency of three dimensions is "triadox." Anna beautifully paints the picture of our human triadox – mind, body, and spirit – as an interwoven fabric that covers us with grace and peace. Anna reveals her expertise and passion within all three dimensions in order to create 3D harmony in our lives. The tension of our mind, body, and spirit triadox is the power Anna describes that allows us to achieve optimal health and wellbeing.

Anna's giftedness is being able to see with her mind's eye, speak with her body's voice, and listen with her spirit's ear. This triadoxical gift engages, empowers, and encourages through-out her message. All of us will benefit from The Intellect of the Mind, Body, and Spirit as it reflects the triadox that Anna has for us all: a life of health, happiness, and hope. Thank you, Anna, for the blessings of your life and for sharing those blessings with us.

> Dr. Gary Gray
> Founder of the Gray Institute

INTRODUCTION

Our healthcare system has mastered interventions in treating patient conditions and saving lives through our talented and skillful practitioners and technological advancements. However, the way we traditionally treat the physical manifestation of diseases and injuries emphasizes a highly reactive approach through surgery, physical therapy, and a plethora of prescription medications. We turn to pharmaceuticals to ease our pain, relieve our anxiety, help us sleep, keep us focused, keep us happy, and keep us alive. Then, we resort to more medications to undo the side effects of the preceding ones.

While this approach is a vital component in maintaining our health, the key to the optimal quality of life we all hope for is a heavier emphasis on the prevention of disease. Before we can expect to see our healthcare system shift its priorities to preventative solutions, we must make our own commitment to prevention—from within. Through a team approach with our dedicated healthcare providers, we can achieve our optimal quality of life without the physical and financial consequences we experience today.

People commonly believe that the ailments they experience today and will surely experience in the future are due to genetics. On the contrary, I believe we have far more power over our health. We don't have to anticipate some inevitable health issue just because our parents and grandparents had it. Dr. Suhas Kshirsagar phrased it perfectly at an event I attended at the Chopra Center when he said, "Genetics is like a loaded gun. It is your lifestyle that pulls the trigger."

As I write this, it's the year 2020, which has truly been a symbolically visionary year. In order to remain grounded during the Covid-19 pandemic or any other form of turbulence, we need a solid foundation. Many of us found that we were ill-prepared for it physically, financially, professionally, mentally, emotionally, or all of the above. Covid-19 is not our first "storm" and will likely not be our last. Every time a new crisis arises, we can take shelter as we look for new vaccines, medications, or protective gear. But ultimately, we need to ensure a solid foundation in mind, body, and spirit to bulletproof our lives and well-being through these unprecedented times.

Who Are You?

Are you the voice in your head? The physical being that does, does, does and goes, goes, goes? Are you a non-tangible spirit or energy source?

Over the past twenty-two years of studying wellness during undergraduate, graduate, and post-doctorate studies, I have come to fully appreciate that true wellness is multifaceted. Our mind, body, and spirit encompass the three aspects of our human experience, and they are fully interdependent. We need good health in all three if we are to achieve optimal fitness, longevity, and inner peace.

I often observe people emphasizing their physical well-being while they neglect their mind and spirit. This leaves them unfulfilled from the physical achievements they manage to reach. Then, there are those who emphasize their spiritual path with constant meditation and solitude while they give little regard to their physical health or human existence. Then, we see the people who fully capitalize on their mind's intellectual capacity, even revered for their worldly inventions, but they feel empty in the physical and spiritual aspects of their lives.

As French Philosopher Pierre Teilhard de Chardin famously said, "We are not human beings having a spiritual experience. We are spiritual beings having a human experience." Our purpose is to enjoy, embrace, and participate in life, appreciating the journey within the context of mind, body, and spirit alike- the three fundamental dimensions of living.

We aren't here to exclusively meditate our life away in the mountains, nor are we here to abuse our bodies by chasing after an elusive time in our youth when we felt most valued. But wait: is wishing to be beautiful, fit, and youthful at any age wrong? And haven't the spiritual teachings of the ages traditionally taught us to reject the body and worldly desires?

If we place our value solely on our physicality from a younger time, it can take away from our limitless potential today. If we instead set an intention to remain healthy, exude beauty and fitness, and stay aligned with the joy of life, we will add to our spiritual experience as we reinvent ourselves at every stage of living. It's imperative to understand that we're either flourishing, or we're wilting. Each of us must change, expand, and evolve to keep the life force flowing through us. There is no need to waste time getting attached to anything positive or negative in our existence—all of it will change. In fact, the only constant that exists is change itself.

That isn't a negative phenomenon. Just as the iPhone craze would be long forgotten had it never evolved past iPhone version 2, our spiritual evolution instinctively expects a better and better version of ourselves in every stage of our ever-changing existence.

You are here to radiate the highest expressions from your mind, body, and spirit in perfect harmony and balance. This space of perfect alignment is where your optimal health, inner and outer beauty, inner and outer peace, and inner and outer brilliance resides.

What To Expect From This Book

As a Doctor of Physical Therapy and a wellness expert, I'm writing this book from my training and experience in the medical field, as well as my continuing education in Ayurvedic principles, nutrition, meditation, and also my personal life experience.

First, I will dive deep into how to prevent and heal musculoskeletal injuries optimally, improve sports performance for all ages and all levels, lose weight safely, eat healthy, and age gracefully. I will also cover how to have a healthy pregnancy.

Beyond the body, however, I will go into important mind and spirit wellness topics such as the mind and body connection, mindfulness, abundances, oneness, our children, and even our end of life transition.

This book is truly a holistic journey to help you integrate general well-being of mind, body, and spirit and improve self-love, health, longevity, and inner peace. My sincerest hope is that these pages will help you maximize compassion, forgiveness, and understanding for yourself and others, live with greater purpose, and experience profound joy and happiness.

CHAPTER ONE

Follow Your Inner Voice

When I was fourteen years old, my best friend Sarah was hospitalized with meningitis and went into a coma. After two weeks, the hospital staff began to give up, saying that even if she woke up, she would be a "vegetable" due to brain damage. The medical team told her parents that they believed it was time to stop intervening.

When Sarah's parents refused to end life support for their child, the medical staff in-formed them that insurance would stop paying for her care. Naturally, her mom and dad were devastated, but they couldn't bring themselves to give up on their daughter. It just didn't feel "right." With no other options left, they reached out for spiritual help. This isn't uncommon in times of crisis when our physical capabilities are lessened.

Through a family member, they connected with a known healer, who asked for a picture of Sarah to pray over. Her parents immediately obliged and organized a prayer healing session over the phone.

Concurrently, a physician in the hospital was arguing with the medical team that she felt a specific medication could remedy Sarah's condition, but she was vetoed by all of the other doctors. The night after the prayer session had taken place, this physician was on call, so she started the medication on Sarah despite the other doctors' objections.

By the next morning, a shocked nurse scrambled to corral the medical staff into Sarah's room. She had opened her eyes and started talking after more than two weeks in a coma.

We visited Sarah the day she woke up, and my mother recalls, still in disbelief: "Not only was she talking, but she couldn't stop talking. She kept talking about the Pope coming to visit her the night before. She talked about being hungry and wanting a hamburger. It was nonstop rambling, but we were in tears of joy to see her well again."

After this miraculous recovery, there was a debate among Sarah's family and others around her about what had "cured" her. Was it the spiritual healer? Was it the prayers and the faith of the parents? Was it the dedicated physician who matched my friend's needs perfectly with the right medication? Or was its pure coincidence?

These teachings suggest *all of the above*. A mind, body, spirit phenomenon occurred when a family's collective desire created the perfect physical behaviors and perfect scenario (the enlightened physician who found herself with the opportunity to take a chance) to heal their child—all driven by a higher consciousness through original will.

The result: "prayers answered."

There are many miraculous stories that speak volumes about the importance of listening to our innate wisdom within. After that incident, Sarah became a more faith-based person. In adulthood, she first became a nurse and later went further to graduate from medical school. Clearly, the prophecy of the disbelieving physicians that this young lady would turn into a "vegetable" upon awakening was refuted by her ability to live her life purpose today as a physician serving others.

In physical therapy school, I recall our professor saying to our class, "You will see people in very extreme circumstances during your practice. Sometimes, they'll have cancer or some other life-threatening condition. Whatever you do, do not give your patients false hope. Do not tell them everything is okay when it isn't just to make them feel better." There are valid reasons why healthcare providers are told not to, and why they do not for the most part, give hope to patients in very bleak circumstances. For one, we would not want a patient to lose their compliance with their medical orders under a false premise that they are "fine." We would like to avoid the feeling of letting someone down if everything does not turn out okay, especially if we have had that experience in the past with another patient who did not recover well. There can also be some fear of responsibility and liability that may come with giving a patient "false hope." However, I have learned that it isn't necessarily my responsibility to *remove* someone's hope or faith that they may heal either, regardless of their circumstances. In all my years of practice and in my one-year observation at an ICU department, I can tell you that miracles happen more often than I once thought possible. As one of my patients told me with a big grin after overcoming stage four cancer, "When Western technology meets Eastern philosophy, magic happens." This patient followed all medical advice and added to that a holistic approach to change her lifestyle, meditation, and even energy healing sessions called Reiki. Even as the most educated healthcare providers, we must remain humble and acknowledge that we do not have a magic ball to predict every direction a patient's health can take them, for better or for worse. In my observation, the patients who overcame tremendous odds held a strong belief and will that they would overcome their circumstances. They did their due diligence to help themselves from a healthcare standpoint and remained in a state of detachment from outcome versus a state of fear or desperation. In this space of strong will, action, and indomitable spirit, these patients made me a believer that we can at times change the fabric of reality.

My intention in telling you this story and in writing this book is to help you tap into the unlimited potential of your mind, body, and spirit to guide you. This book is created as a reminder that your health, purpose, and future well-being are purely at your own discretion. It's a reminder to follow your inner voice, to write your own story, and to refuse to allow anyone else to dictate what you do or believe. Your body will always work toward its most healthy and ideal state, as long as you don't interfere with its ability to do so.

The Limitless Mind: We are All a Genius at Some Level

The statement that we're all a genius at some level isn't advocacy for a "celebration of mediocrity"—it's based on scientific research. Many patients and individuals I've spoken with aren't familiar with the work of Dr. Howard Gardner, a professor at Harvard University. Dr. Garner theorized that although we only acknowledge two types of intelligence (linguistic and logical) in school and classroom settings, there are actually eight forms of intelligence that we use in life. Generally speaking, those who are strong in those two standard areas (or who can get there with great effort) are esteemed, and those who cannot are labeled as having learning disabilities.

This observation that many various forms of

intelligence exist among us, whether appreciated or not, is ingenious. I see these various types of intelligence displayed in my patients daily. Here is the multiple intelligence list from the work of Dr. Gardner:

1. Words (linguistic Intelligence)

2. Numbers or logic (logical intelligence)

3. Pictures (visual-spatial intelligence)

4. Music (musical intelligence)

5. Self-Reflection (intra-personal intelligence)

6. Physical (bodily-kinesthetic intelligence)

7. Social intelligence (interpersonal skills/intelligence)

8. Natural world (naturalist intelligence)

There are many great examples of this to discuss, but I'll mention just a couple to give you a better understanding of this concept. I had a patient who complained to me that his brother had always been the "C" student in the family who struggled immensely just to achieve a passing grade. "I was the one who achieved straight As in school and barely had to try to get them," my patient told me. "Ironically, my brother is the one who has the hotshot job and all the money and high lifestyle everyone thought I would have. Well, I know why. He has this personality type that people gravitate to, and that's something I just never had. People love to be around him all the time. He seems to always know exactly what to say. I just never knew how to connect with people like he did."

This patient is a great example of someone who has

perhaps the first two types of intelligence while his brother has strong social intelligence. The ability to read people's facial expressions, understand where they're coming from, and recognize what's bothering them without their having to spell it out is a form of social intelligence that not everyone has.

Of course, just because you have great social intelligence, it doesn't necessarily mean you'll have poor logical intelligence or poor representations of any of the other types. Our strengths and biases may present in many variations.

As another example, let's consider a high-level athlete who is flunking out of school. Sadly, there's a label created for this stereotype: "The Dumb Jock." Interestingly, a science teacher may view this person as a lost cause, but he's actually a genius in motor intelligence.

Every motor movement we initiate is a connection between the brain and our muscles to execute the movement, ideally without error or injury. Physical performance isn't independent of the use and acuity of the brain. This science teacher judging the "dumb jock" may fall flat on their face trying to do a fraction of what the motor genius athlete can do. The logical intelligence-dominant teacher could train their whole life and never gain the ability to perform a fraction of what a physical intelligence-dominant athlete performs effortlessly.

I'm embarrassed to say that we even have a term in the physical therapy world for patients who are so low on the motor intelligence scale that they can't learn one basic motor task. This makes progress in therapy very difficult. The term is "motor idiot," a derogatory one that I personally refrain from using. But I've heard other physical therapists complain, "My patient is such a motor idiot.

We've practiced the same movement one hundred times, and he acts like it's the first time he's ever done it." These patients who struggle with motor movements are often highly intelligent individuals from a words and numbers perspective. They're simply not as strong in motor intelligence. That said, if you have ever been wrongly accused of being a "dumb jock," you now know you can counter that statement with, "at least my physical therapist would never call me a motor idiot." Clearly, I'm joking here, as I would ultimately wish that every person, every teacher, and every mentor acknowledge and appreciate the gifts that each individual brings, as we all contribute to society greatly. And all of these types of intelligence are equally necessary.

You also know when you meet someone who is using their particular genius to great advantage. Have you ever received some form of service from someone, and you knew immediately that this person was living their life purpose? You felt in awe at their knowledge, skillfulness, and happiness in their profession. Even if they worked long hours, they probably said something like, "I enjoy this so much that it doesn't feel like work to me."

When we're aligned with our gifts and passions, what we do doesn't feel like a job. And the kind of service doesn't matter. It can be a charismatic server at a restaurant, a knowledgeable mechanic, or an inspirational teacher.

We all certainly know the difference between someone like that and someone who is clearly miserable in their field of choice. When we find purpose in what we truly enjoy that uses our natural genius, we exude a vibration that's irresistible to the world. We become a magnet to abundance, which aligns us with expansion and the success that follows.

Of course, to increase and maintain our innate areas of intelligence, it's important to exercise our brains just as we exercise our bodies. What we don't value and use will atrophy, and that includes the brain. A book called *Super Brain: Unleashing the Explosive Power of Your Mind to Maximize Health, Happiness, and Spiritual Well-Being* by Deepak Chopra, M.D. and Rudolphe E. Tanzi, Ph.D. provides great insight about the importance of creating new neural networks throughout our life to maintain our level of acuity well into our older years. They discuss the fact that Albert Einstein's brain was found to be 10 percent smaller than the average brain and showed no unusual features to explain his brilliance.

Einstein frequently attributed his success to his thirst for knowledge and discovery. So avoiding autopilot by creating new adventures in your life is the pathway to a sound and high functioning brain. Aging of our brain is indeed caused by disuse more than by time elapsed.

In physical therapy, we see the value in creating new neural pathways when we work with patients who experienced a stroke, traumatic brain injury, or some other nerve injury. We have come a long way in learning how to help our patients by challenging them to use the injured limb and encourage neuroplasticity or rewire the brain to recover movement and function through the compensation of helpful neighboring cells.

With all of this value in challenging our minds, the next time you feel stressed about having to learn a new skill or change an activity, remind yourself that you're providing the highest quality nourishment to your brain despite the fears you may feel about it. Complacency and boredom will be the ultimate insult to the long-term growth and health of your brain.

CHAPTER TWO

Musculoskeletal Well-Being

I will now dig into my "bread and butter" and talk about the ideal physical therapy experience and musculoskeletal health/maintenance. The magic happens when patients and therapists work as a team to conquer hurdles and achieve the desired results together. I value a therapist who thinks critically, not just treating the injury, but delving in like a human mechanic to find what caused the body part to fail. This helps to identify the root cause and establish injury pre-vention for patients.

Let's start with a few concepts to understand how the body gets into "trouble" in the first place.

The Happy Middle

If we did everything in moderation, we would rarely encounter a problem. If we sat in moderation, exercised in moderation, ate in moderation, rested in moderation, slept in moderation, stressed in moderation, and drank alcohol in moderation, we would rarely have issues come up from any of these actions.

Even good things should be done in moderation. If we look at marathon runners—the ones we all applaud for their ability to persevere at such great lengths of continuous running—we find that they're more susceptible to injuries and burnout because a marathon isn't a moderate undertaking. They encounter more muscle imbalances, repetitive use injuries/stress fractures, and a lower immune system, leaving them also more susceptible to illnesses. For the longevity of their health and the ability to continue running, they must be mindful of when it's time to train and when it's time to rest. And if you're feeling ill, don't fall for the false assumption that going to the gym to "sweat it out" will help you recover faster. To fight pathogens, your body prefers to shut down to focus its energy on the war going on internally. Does this mean no one should aim high and achieve excellence in sports or hobbies? Certainly not. There is merit and value in everything we set out to achieve and experience in our lives. However, it isn't the path to longevity, nor is it sustainable, for your body to be in a state of constant overexertion.

After taking a cross-fit type of workout class at a gym, my husband and I chatted with the young, fit instructor about her personal workouts and accomplishments. She looked disappointed as she explained to us how she used to train excessively hard and was able to qualify for the Boston Marathon, only to have to stop due to hip fractures and other severe injuries. But she only experienced hip stress fractures at such a young age from the excessive challenges that her mind placed on her body. It wasn't sustainable. This young lady had the talent and drive, and she may have been able to participate in high level sports activities she enjoyed for far longer if she'd done so with a balance of rest, mindfulness, and moderation.

So as you reflect on your diet, physical activity, and general lifestyle, what could you change to find your happy middle?

The Path of Least Resistance

In a flowing river, the water follows the path of least resistance. Our bodies work in a similar fashion. When there's too much resistance in the path intended, such as limited motion due to a stiff joint, the human body will borrow from a more willing path or more mobile part of the body in order to make that intended movement.

Since today's world comes with technological advancements that leave many of us sitting extensively for work, school, gaming, and internet shopping, etc., these kinds of compensations are rampant. The areas of our bodies that are most susceptible to stiffness due to sitting at devices are the thoracic spine (upper back), the hip joint, and the ankle joint. Gravity further reinforces this phenomenon when we give in to it by rounding our shoulders forward, causing excessive kyphosis (rounding) of our upper back. This forward flexed position or poor postural awareness causes imbalances and stiffness throughout the body, most prominently of the chest muscles and the front aspect of our hips referred to as the "hip flexors."

These muscles tighten and literally shorten with prolonged sitting, causing an array of issues with muscle weakness and altered body mechanics. Most of the joints in our extremities operate much like a pulley system, where various muscles orchestrate a proper movement pattern. When our pulley system is off balance due to poor posture, the joint develops equally poor tracking. Hence, wear and tear, as well as inflammation, will result over time.

For example, a golfer who is swinging a club will ideally

use motion predominantly through the hip and thoracic spine (upper back). But golfers often twist excessively through their lumbar spine during their swing due to inadequate range of motion in the thoracic spine and/or in the hip joint, leaving their unstable but more mobile lumbar spine to do more of the twisting. This is a very common reason why golfers complain of back pain or lumbar radiculitis (irritated nerve in the leg/s) following a round of golf.

We also see the path of least resistance in other sports and other joints. We sometimes feel pain during the simple act of walking due to this phenomenon.

Everything is Connected

As you start to lose movement in one plane of motion, you may soon start to lose it in the other planes, as well as in adjacent or distant structures of your body. This is because every part is connected and harmonious in its ideal state. You may notice once your posture is flexed forward, not only have you lost the motion and strength to straighten back up, but you now have difficulty rotating and bending your upper back to the side as well. You will most likely notice you can't raise your arm overhead as high as you used to.

Try this test for yourself. Stand erect with your shoulders back and your chest out. Now, raise your arm over your head. Get a feel for how high your arm is able to elevate overhead and the level of effort it takes to raise your arm up high. Next, slump your upper back, and round your shoulders forward. Try to elevate your shoulders again while remaining in this slumped position. The vast majority of you will have a much harder time, and possibly even experience pain, when raising your arm as high as in the first scenario. This is because your slumped upper back has limited the ability of your shoulder to elevate your arm overhead fully without causing structures in your shoulders to jam together. The harmonious movement that needs to occur between your shoulder joint, thoracic joints, and shoulder blades to allow the pulley system of your shoulder to function optimally is blocked by the slumped posture.

In general, every movement lends motion up or down the chain to allow for basic activities such as proper gait, proper loading, or proper motion. Even losing the harmonious swing of our arms while walking can cause an array of immobility issues through the upper back, hips, ankles, and neck.

If you're a runner and have severely limited neck motion, your shoulders won't be able to rotate adequately to allow running without neck pain. If your ankle motion is limited or you have excessive motion, it can cause abnormal movement of your hips, resulting in persistent hip pathologies that don't respond well to hip treatment alone.

I recommend consulting a physical therapist who knows their biomechanics well if you have persistent hip pain that hasn't responded to an isolated hip rehab program. I have had countless ankle and foot cases that were unresponsive to injections, orthotics, casting, and physical therapy for the foot. But they quickly responded to treatments of the hip and core in addition to a foot/ankle program. The ankle and foot may be on the receiving end of the pain, though not necessarily the cause of the pain.

Lifting 1,000 Pounds with One Buddy . . . or a Large Group of Buddies

As we start losing motion and the efficiency of our body, some of our muscles become minimally active while some become overly dominant. This can occur with repetitive lifting activities, where we continue to use the same movement pattern and favor certain muscles over and over again.

These muscle imbalances cause a dysfunction of the pulley system and the harmony that exists within our normal movement, eventually resulting in injury. For example, if you're lifting a box, you can bend over at the waist and round your shoulders to lift the box. This is a common way to go about it, but it's highly inefficient.

Alternatively, you can recruit exponentially more "friends" or muscle groups to help with the lift by squatting properly to allow your powerful bottom muscles to assist and then pinch the shoulder blades back to engage some of the muscles in the back of your shoulders in addition to your chest muscles. You can further lighten that effort by pulling in your lower abdominal muscles to help stabilize, balance, and protect your spine while you lift.

Even the basic movement of raising your arm overhead requires a series of muscles to orchestrate proper form for elevation that we term "scapulohumeral rhythm." When we have muscle imbalances surrounding the shoulder girdle, this rhythm is disrupted, and we're unable to recruit all of the muscles required to lift our arms without pain. This is what I refer to as inviting a crew to help you lift versus overextending a mere couple of muscle groups. You may also add in physics principles to make the weight of the box feel like quite a bit less by keeping the box as close to you as possible when lifting.

Now that you know some of the basics of how

the body works and gets into "trouble," let's talk about sports performance.

CHAPTER THREE

Sports Performance

You're only as strong as you are flexible. The "load and explode" principle is key to every human movement, though even more pronounced during sports performance. Movements during sports typically require far greater power, velocity, and flexibility. I like the analogy of Dr. Gary Gray, one of the pioneers of Applied Functional Science and founder of the Gray Institute, on this topic. He explains the thinking of your muscles like a slingshot. The further you pull your rubber band, the further your rock will fly. The less pull or stretch available in your rubber band, the less powerful/effective your shot will be.

To achieve the highest sports performance or any human movement, your muscles must load properly. This will require adequate availability of motion at the joint level and flexibility of the muscles/tissue. For example, let's look at the movement of jumping. To get the highest jump possible, it's imperative to squat low enough to load your gluteal (bottom) muscles and your quads (thigh muscles) before exploding upright and into the air. This is the stretch leading to a spring mechanism that we refer to as lengthening a muscle in order to load it for optimal muscle performance. Unfortunately, many people don't squat or train low enough to fully lengthen the gluteal muscles in order to load or strengthen them through their full range.

Squatting too low has its own inefficiency and injury susceptibility issues, however. Again, there's a "happy middle" here. Still, most of the time, people are more inclined to not squat low enough than to squat too low.

If we don't have that motion available due to injury, tightness, poor posture, or excessive sitting during the day, that loss of motion will result in improper loading, injury, or simply less ideal muscle performance.

Training Should Be Sport or Activity-Specific

All too often, I see athletes spend extensive time training their muscles in a way that doesn't simulate human movement. Our gluteal muscles do abduct our hip (move the leg away from the midline) when we lie down on our sides. But they play a much different role in running and walking, as they stabilize and manage ground reaction forces to help propel us forward.

Most therapists and physicians agree that patients rarely come into our offices and say they injured themselves while lying down on their side. Most often, accidents happen when people are upright and bearing weight. Therefore, it's vital for injury prevention and superior sports performance to train in a way that's more authentic to how we move and to the circumstances that make us most vulnerable to injury.

"Proprioception" is the body's ability to know spatially where each limb/body part exists in space in order to react quickly when we tread on non-advantageous grounds. A soccer player, for example, will need to use extraordinary proprioception to maneuver a soccer ball, guard the ball by quickly moving its location, and dodge competitors while running on uneven surfaces at high speed-all without spraining an ankle. Of course, not all of these maneuvers are done in one straight line down a field. Our proprioceptors become even more stimulated when we quickly change directions. In this example, a soccer player will be moving forwards or backwards in a straight plane (termed the sagittal plane), side to side (termed frontal plane) and sometimes in rotational movements such as pivoting and twisting (termed the transverse plane). It is imperative to recognize that our world is three-dimensional and, therefore, our training should be too.

Yet, despite all these dynamic movements that are so evident in sports and basic human movement, many athletes spend too much time on weight machines that are non-weight-bearing during their training. This means that they sit on a seat or lie down on a bench, working their muscles in non-functional methods. Does this create hypertrophy or enlargement of the muscles? Sure. Does it create more strength in the muscles? Likely. But does it improve functional muscle and sports performance and serve as an injury prevention method? Probably not.

Seated, isolated muscle training will not excite or train your proprioceptors nor utilize three-dimensional movements that are true to sports and human function. You can check someone's strength while they lie down on a table, and they may demonstrate a maximum muscle strength rating when they push or resist against your hand (our traditional method of manual muscle-testing). But when you ask them to stand up and load their weight on that joint and muscle, you may find that the joint and muscle aren't strong enough for the person's body weight. The muscle reaction time may also be insufficient when they're managing human movement in standing positions.

Dr. Gray has had in-depth discussions on the importance of all of these fundamental concepts in sports—in particular, training more authentically to human movement in three-dimensional planes. The Gray Institute website is accessible to anyone interested in learning more about biomechanics.

Going Back Too Soon

The patients who have the quickest and most ideal outcomes realize the need to change habits and work on their areas of weakness before returning to previous activities. Some athletes are fully attached to their former workouts because they had success with them in the past despite the injuries and undesirable circumstance they've experienced from them. While therapy can still do wonders in helping an athlete balance out weaknesses and manage an injury while continuing to play or train, the ideal choice is to remove the body from the state of stress and inflammatory cycle. This allows a clean slate in building a stronger foundation more quickly with better long-term results.

The saying, "old habits die hard" accurately describes the brain's tendency to adopt persistent faulty movement patterns and ingrain them as the new normal. Fortunately, this plasticity of the brain also works in our favor in the rehabilitation process as we can instill new motor patterns. It becomes much easier to establish and reinforce new patterns without interference and hindrance from former compensation patterns when we work within a controlled rehab program.

Essentially, my advice is: don't go back too soon to your former activities! Be patient. Typically, the pain goes away much faster than strength and stability is restored. So you may get ahead of yourself by going back to high-level activities before it's advisable for your body. Enjoy pain-free movements for at least a couple of weeks before testing the waters (with your therapist's blessing that you're ready). Then, return to your sport goals better prepared for success.

Should I Stretch Before a Game or Not?

This question has caused an ongoing debate for decades. There is literature out there that runners who do extensive stretching tend to have more injuries and pain afterward. Some believe that prolonged stretching causes the muscles and proprioceptors to turn off, leaving us more vulnerable to an injury during a sport. The debate about long-held stretches versus ballistic stretching (bouncing in and out of a stretch) has flip-flopped back and forth, leaving many athletes unsure of how to prepare for their race or game. The answer to this is: your stretch should be sport-specific, just as your training and rehab program should be sport-specific.

1. Stretches should be in three planes of motion, as sports will require your muscles to pivot, cut, and stretch in all three dimensions of movement.

2. Stretches before a game should ideally be done while in functional /weight-bearing (standing) positions. This will excite your proprioceptors while you stretch.

3. The stretches you choose should mimic your sport. Since most sports are quick movements, your stretch shouldn't necessarily be "bouncy," though it shouldn't be a long hold either. Ideally, you will move in and out of the stretch and gently work into stretching further. But listen to your body. There's a difference between the natural discomfort of stretching deeper than normal versus the pain of passing beyond the limits of your muscles.

I also factor in if patients have a neural or nerve type of injury. Nerves don't respond well to long-held stretches. Such stretches reduce the blood flow and tend to irritate the nerve further rather than help it to heal. Once aggravated, this neural tension can reduce your range of motion along the nerve pathway.

4. Long-held stretches will cause more lengthening and changes in the tissue, which may be necessary in patients with extensively shortened muscles. I recommend this stretch only for certain patients following their sports activities or as part of their rehab program, though typically not before they go out to play.

Once you achieve the increased motion and muscle length desired through stretching, it's important to add strengthening and stability exercises through your newfound range of motion. Some therapists are surprised as they explain, "I helped the patient get all this new motion, and then they didn't come back for a few weeks. When they returned, they said they felt a lot worse than before." This is because the increased mobility these patients gained needed to be kept in check with more stability. The new motion is uncharted ground where proprioceptors are still in a learning phase, resulting in more awkward movements than the smaller range of motion they had before. The newfound range needs to be trained and controlled. This can occur in the neck, hip, or any other part of the body. If you gain a lot of motion in your knee and then lunge forward into that new range immediately, you may find that your knee feels a little wobbly, or it may even slightly buckle and feel less controlled.

This is when athletes sometimes return to their sport with more motion but feel worse due to the lack of control they have over the motion they gained. I recommend training in the deeper ranges with your therapist, guiding you to keep the motion gradual, safe, and pain-free.

CHAPTER FOUR

Combating Sedentary Lifestyles

With increasing numbers of us leading sedentary lifestyles both at work and at home, our bodies feel stiff and out of balance. Those of us who sit most of the day at work are turning off our rear hip muscles and tightening our front hip flexors. While in sitting positions, our upper back becomes rounded and stiff, while our neck is in an awkward position.

On the weekends, some of us want to make up for lost time during the week by tackling the gym or participating in other physical activities. Unfortunately, since our bodies have been stiffening all week, we're ill-prepared for the range of motion, load, or stress that we ask of our joints and soft tissue over the weekend.

This is why we simply must avoid keeping our muscles in the same position for hours. We have to make time throughout the day at work to stretch, walk, and move. It will improve blood flow and joint lubrication to inhibit our muscles and joints from stiffening as much.

Regardless of the artificial environments we've created in today's world, our bodies were simply designed to move continuously throughout each day. I recommend that employers consider incorporating movement breaks at work (within reason). What a great way to maintain healthier employees and improve blood flow for better work performance. Teachers may also find that students perform better on tests and schoolwork when they have a break to do five minutes of exercise during each hour.

In the mornings and evenings, I suggest doing some form of exercise that's approved by your physician or physical therapist. On the weekends, of course, you may have more time to invest in an activity, but try moderate exercises, working your way up gradually to higher levels if you wish to push yourself.

Obesity

I'll never forget my 50-year-old patient John, who limped into my clinic at 5'10" and nearly four hundred pounds. Before we even began therapy, he was sweating profusely and short of breath by the time he made it into the treatment room. He told me he was hardly able to get up from his chair due to severe bilateral knee pain. He couldn't get upstairs to sleep in his bed with his wife, who was fit and active. She wanted to travel more, while he was no longer able to leave the house much at all. I listened intently to his goals and concerns as we designed a program unique to him.

With obesity, it usually takes longer for rehab to work due to the irritation from walking, let alone the stiffness from being so sedentary. It took more thought to design a program around his weight, but I had all sorts of ideas for him. We spent a couple of days performing exercises, and I could tell he was doing them at home because I barely had to cue him on the next exercise after we finished the previous one. He sat on the recumbent bike and needed frequent breaks to get to a mere five minutes, but he was determined to complete every task. "I can't believe I'm already noticing less knee pain after just a couple of sessions," he told me. "I'm already walking around the house more."

"I can tell you're working hard on the program, and I'm very impressed with your progress and diligence," I responded. To my surprise, he teared up and proceeded to tell me how scared he had been to start therapy, not knowing what to expect. He proceeded to tell me that he was embarrassed and ashamed of himself for being so big. He was afraid I would criticize him or send him back home, saying there was no hope for him and that he'd eventually be stuck in a wheelchair.

As sentimental as I am, I had to push back a few tears to keep my composure as I told him, "You had a choice to not show up for therapy at all. You could have chosen not to do your exercises at home, too. You could have given up and taken the easier route, but you didn't take the easy route, did you? You worked hard and are already seeing differences in standing up with less knee pain. You have newfound hope, and I'm proud of you."

It was one of the most eye-opening moments in my career, as I hadn't yet fully appreciated how much fear someone can feel on the other side of therapy as a patient. John worked hard every day and every session as we saw his endurance and stamina improve on the recumbent bike. His workouts progressed to full weight-bearing, squats, lunges, balance activities, and core exercises. There was a lot of sweat in his rehab program, but the tears became more from joy than shame or fear. John achieved his goals of climbing the stairs to access his bedroom and keeping up with his wife on outings. Most importantly, he gained confidence in his abilities.

All of us can have tremendous success just by taking

the first step to being more active and setting our intention on our desired outcomes. Success begets more success. As you start to feel better and less in pain, you will feel freer to exercise more and more. You may start to enjoy how it feels to be stronger and decide to talk to a dietician or your doctor about a diet that will help you with weight loss (if weight is an issue for you).

Once John got past his feelings of self-judgment, his momentum changed direction so that he became unstoppable. This is my hope for anyone who feels their weight gain is hindering their goals and taking away from their quality of life.

Physical therapy is highly effective for obese individuals. A therapist's encouragement and resources for an obese patient to move past this hurdle are invaluable.

Physical Activity/Walks

During an exercise science class at Kansas University, I was flabbergasted when our professor told us that human beings were intended to have at least eight hours of physical activity per day! Who gets even close to that anymore? Maybe farmers and shepherds (in fact, shepherds are some of the world's longest living individuals), whose activity level stays at a moderate intensity all day long. Unlike these remarkable people, the majority of us are sitting all day at work or in a car or airplane. A few of us may get some form of mild to intense workout at the gym after work.

Most of us are unable to pursue a career as a shepherd, but we can try growing our own garden and using fewer creature comforts such as garage door openers, golf carts, elevators and cars when it's safe and feasible to walk. We can also play outside with our kids, which is good for both our health and our children's health, as kids spend too much time on electronics, too. Outdoor activities surrounded by nature have been proven to reduce incidents of psychological/depressive episodes in children.

Taking walks has been associated with better heart and brain health, mood, joint motion and lubrication, standing balance, and balanced spinal disc fluids. Daily walks are actually one of the best preventative tools we have available to us. No machinery required!

Dancing is also one of the most therapeutic activities for your mind, body, and spirit. But choose any activity that lifts your spirits on a given day. It doesn't have to be preplanned like a chore. Recently, I have switched to this method as part of my mindfulness practice. I like to cycle, run with my dogs, hike, dance, lift weights, do a home boot camp-type class that I created, and swim. Some days, I feel my body needs rest, so I take walks, which are less demanding. Each day, I ask myself what feels best to my mind, body, and spirit, and I let the answer inspire me.

Some of you may feel you need a more organized regimen, such as classes that keep you accountable and give you the added benefit of socialization. The key is to find what works for you and to keep moving prudently and mindfully with your wellness at heart.

You could even invite a love interest/partner to exercise with you. Did you know that working out with someone else is a great way to enhance your physical attraction toward one another? A Harvard graduate psychology professor I had at KU shared research with us that found while people are exercising, they view other people within their line of vision as far more attractive than if they saw them at a time that was not during their workout. It's similar to what we refer to as wearing "beer goggles" when people start to look more attractive after we've had a few drinks. So grab your love interest, and get moving together!

There's a "use it or lose it principle" at play here. What you give attention to grows and flourishes. What you neglect, wilts. I don't believe we get "old" and become less active. I believe that becoming less active leads to feeling old and then growing old. In other words, we age when we stop living.

Postural Alignment

Since posture is such a common problem, what can you do about it? Anthropology studies have found that human beings were created as an endurance species, not as sitting athletes! Sitting isn't natural to our bodies, so we should minimize the amount of time we spend in a chair or couch. If you must sit or have to look down at a computer, I suggest spending your time outside of work undoing the stagnant, flexed forward positions that sitting creates.

Many of us have kids who sit all day in school and then come home to spend the rest of the evening on electronics. I have never seen so many kids with headaches and stiff joints in their spine than I have in this day and age. I recommend minimizing their continuous time on electronics in a sitting position.

Use lunch breaks to lie down on a foam roll and stretch out your chest and shoulder muscles. This is highly beneficial in resolving the stiffness that sets in after continuous hours at your desk. Even a short walk during your lunch break to lubricate your joints and release tension in your hips can be highly beneficial. This also takes pressure off of the discs in your lumbar spine that experience three times more stress in sitting than in any other position.

For your neck and shoulders, movement in your upper back and neck is the key. Practice pinching your shoulder blades together by rotating your shoulders back without allowing your shoulders to rise up or down. This will activate your posture muscles between your shoulder blades and hinder your ability to slouch. By keeping your chin tucked, your ears will align with your shoulders and reduce the effort required by the cervical extensor muscles to keep your head in a neutral position.

But I don't advise walking around like a stiff robot all day! Simply check in and ensure that your head isn't constantly forward. If so, you may want to go to a wall and practice aligning the back of your body, the back of your arms, and the base of your head to the wall. To balance out some of your postural weaknesses, hold that position until you feel fatigue between your shoulder blades. Following this activity, add in functional movements by slowly reaching overhead and across your body in different directions to lengthen the muscles that have tightened while you were seated. Of course, all exercises and stretches should be done in a pain-free range. When you start to feel pain, don't stretch further.

Balance

Just as ideal posture may escape us, we can also lose our balance over time. This loss may be even more elusive since we can't visibly see the regression occur. As we become more contained at our desk jobs, more predictable in our routines, or just plain sedentary, it's important to incorporate balance exercises into our day to maintain a safe level of stability in the future. The healthcare costs associated with falls are so exorbitant that for quite some time during my practice, Medicare required a balance screening and fall assessment on every Medicare patient who walked through our doors. This was true even if their injury obviously had nothing to do with balance issues. We were then required to incorporate balance therapy into our program should we see deficits that predicted a likelihood of future falls (in addition to the original reason the patient came in for therapy). The good news is that balance training in therapy is likely covered by insurance in most cases. Athletes also benefit from balance training for the enhancement of sports performance. They can work with a PT to obtain a customized balance program, whether for golf, high velocity sports, or even baseball, which requires superior balance and core strength for optimal execution of a simple throw. The sports training aspect may or may not be covered by insurance, but it's often covered when included with treatment for an injury.

Many therapists are now accepting patients through a route termed "Self-Pay," which means treatment without the assistance of medical insurance. The benefit of this is that there is no "middleman" adding stipulations on the length of time of the therapy, the number of visits covered, and the interventions permitted. Most of the time, self-pay therapy also allows therapists to spend an hour "one-on-one" versus having overlap with other patients or provide an abbreviated session of thirty to forty minutes to avoid the overlap. The self-pay route can put you and the therapist in the driver's seat versus your needs being "trumped" by the insurance company's fixation on keeping your expenses as low as possible.

CHAPTER FIVE

Diet and Nourishment

Hippocrates, known as the "Father of Medicine," was a Greek physician born in 460 BC and is one of the most remarkable figures in the history of medicine. His infamous quote, "Let food be thy medicine and medicine be thy food" speaks volumes about the impact of the foods we put into our bodies.

While ideal foods nourish your mind, body, and spirit, poor foods have a slow deteriorating effect. One side effect of a poor diet is increased inflammation within the body. Inflammation can cause significant pain, slow deterioration within your joints and nervous system, and countless other systemic issues and diseases. It can compress nerves and disallow adequate motion within your spine and extremities, affecting your daily function.

During physical therapy rehabilitation for an injury, persistent inflammation can leave you spinning your wheels rather than making strides toward your goals. It slows down muscle activity, hindering your ability to gain the strength and stability necessary to heal and recover. Keeping clear of inflammatory cycles through the right diet and a healthy and active lifestyle is key in the preservation of your musculoskeletal system.

Proper diet and nutrition are also vital to building the muscle mass, strength, and stability necessary to gain the invaluable gift of agility and fitness.

Fad Diets

Why is following a proper diet and staying fit so seemingly elusive these days? The reason why following a proper diet can be complicated in today's world is the overwhelming number of fad diets with conflicting theories. One expert endorses eating as much meat and cheeseburgers as you want, while another says you shouldn't eat anything that comes from an animal. Yet another tells you that you were meant to eat like a caveman. Not only are we left confused, but our body's systems are left disheveled as a result.

During my freshman year at KU, I realized that finding the right diet conducive to health and wellness comes with a learning curve. Young and unassuming, I had believed that any diet plan televised extensively and available at grocery stores was, at minimum, safe to try. Although I was already highly disciplined in favoring healthy foods like vegetables, fruits, and lean proteins (with great results), I decided to try the new diet that everyone was talking about—Atkins. I loaded up on protein and minimized fruits and vegetables.

Incidentally, I was in a Taekwondo class at KU and took an accidental blow to my trunk during a play sparring session after class. I was assessed by a very kind and knowledgeable physician who ordered an x-ray and general bloodwork. At some point later, when we reviewed my results, she explained that I had no serious injuries from the accident, but she found high BUN levels in my bloodwork—a marker of declined kidney health. To my surprise, she asked me, "Are you on that Atkins high protein diet all the kids are on right now?"

"How did she know?" I asked myself. "Yes, I've been trying to follow the recommendations of eating a lot more protein in my diet," I replied sheepishly. It had only been about five weeks since I'd started Atkins.

The physician looked me in the eye and candidly said, "I hate this diet. I really do. I have seen nothing but young adults overextending their kidneys due to all this extra protein they're eating that their body doesn't need and can't handle. They aren't eating enough fruits and vegetables anymore. A good chunk of the weight loss is water weight when you switch to proteins versus carbohydrates. This diet will send you into renal failure and eventually heart failure."

Ironically, when you now look up the cons to this diet more than twenty years later, you find that she was entirely correct. I stopped my high protein diet, and my future kidney lab results normalized. I went back to eating fruits and vegetables in a healthier proportion to protein.

Is this diet entirely "bad" or "wrong"? If you were previously living on processed carbs, candy bars, pasta, and bread, there's something to be gained and weight to be lost from eliminating those foods from your diet. However, in all my years of practice, I have never encountered an obese individual who gained their weight from eating too many carrots or any other fresh vegetable. Have you? We don't tend to overeat those types of foods. Our main food addictions that have been proven to light up the same area of our brains as cocaine are sweets, salt, and fat. This addiction to sweets, salt, and fat that researchers have identified is thought to have been a survival trait that was necessary back when we were hunters and gatherers in the days of scarce food. But it isn't a helpful mechanism in today's world when we're surrounded by fast food restaurants and convenience foods at the grocery stores. You can't stop eating french fries because they have sugar, salt, and fat added to them.

We don't have this issue with a bag of spinach or carrots. There is a "method to the madness" with diets that require extreme food group eliminations. And while they may make you lose weight temporarily, it's time for us to raise our standards to also insist that our goal of weight loss includes enhanced well-being rather than at the expense of our well-being.

Today, there are even more extreme diets coming and going. Many of these fads are based on opinions, and their references are merely anecdotal. Typically, there are no long-term studies completed before claims of effectiveness and safety are made. Similar to smoking, it can take years before a malfunction from a diet can manifest itself and be identified. In hindsight, it was a blessing in disguise to be kicked in the ribs so that I learned quickly about the effects of the diet on my kidneys.

The Blue Zone

Now that we have established the need to exercise caution when starting any new diet, how do you decipher between the conflicting views of experts? After years of research and attending live seminars from world-renowned physicians and dietitians, I have come to embrace what our most reputable experts (mostly) agree on.

One dietary lifestyle I believe is unique and simply brilliant is detailed in a book called *The Blue Zone Solutions* by Dan Buettner. This book stems from a study done on our longest-living people in the world and, even more importantly, the ones demonstrating the greatest quality of life.

I view most tasks in life as skills to acquire. If you want to learn how to become rich, ask someone who's wealthy beyond belief how they attained their abundance. If you want to become better at some sport, follow the path of those who have already been revered for their skillfulness in that particular sport. If you want to learn how to live to be over a hundred and still completely independent, ask the Blue Zone centenarians who are living proof of what works in regard to diet and lifestyle.

This study cross-referenced regions around the world with the largest number of centenarians. Interviews and investigations were conducted to understand their lifestyle and habits in an attempt to identify the common threads in their success.

What I find most unique and valuable, however, is the role diet plays in the lives of these hardy people. Their diet mostly resembles the Mediterranean and Flexitarian diets, which were rated number 1 and number 2 respectively of best diets in the U.S.

The essence of their diet and lifestyle is the practice of simplicity, moderation, sustainability, and responsible practices when raising crops and eating the small amount of meat they include. Most importantly, their *relationship* with food is healthy. I love this idea of starting with our relationship with food.

Are we angry with food for not allowing us to lose weight? Are we stress-eating? Are we eating out of frustration? Or are we eating mindfully and tasting our food, feeling its texture and experiencing fulfillment from it? Are we taking a moment to think about how we feel after we eat, or are we grabbing fast food and scarfing it down mindlessly while hurriedly driving from one appointment to another?

Prior to meeting my husband and starting a family, I would get home from work after a twelve-hour day and eat something so fast that I didn't even take time to sit down. I was eager to get something into my stomach to be able to get to my late-night workout class. Lunch was even worse, as I was often working with my patients during my lunch hour, leaving no more than ten minutes to shovel food into my mouth. Even when I had time to sit down, I would rather stand up at the bar counter and eat fast so that I could move on to my next task.

My husband looked at me like I was a cavewoman and chuckled when I continued this habit for a while after we got married and had kids. It had simply become automatic.

We now enjoy sitting around the table with our large family, elbow to elbow, passing food around to one another. We talk and laugh and comment on our meals. Sometimes, there's a fight over who gets the last roll.

Of course, you don't need a family to eat more mindfully. You can sit down in silence without any screens distracting you. Enjoy the special time dedicated to nourishing your body and stimulating your senses. You will have the same benefits.

In contrast to this common scenario of rushing food in our society, the Blue Zone centenarians' foods are often raised in their personal gardens with a common knowledge of their medicinal capabilities. They treat many of their medical conditions with foods that, for example, lower blood pressure.

Appreciating that we are social creatures, the Blue

Zone individuals are often surrounded by their parents, kids, grandparents, and lifelong friends while they eat and even enjoy a drink or two of alcohol together. Interestingly, the Blue Zone book said that when our kids are surrounded by their grandparents and "family tribe," so to speak, not only does the life expectancy of the grandparents increase, but also the life expectancy of the children and grandchildren. This is something to consider when we reflect on our culture in the United States as the epitome of independence and self-sufficiency.

It isn't uncommon for children to turn eighteen and not just move out, but move across the country and only return for occasional visits. Many times, grandchildren rarely see their grandparents outside of a few special occasions. We're spread out, and regardless of how overextended we are, many of us refuse to accept help from parents and other family members in raising our children. This is a very different philosophy from the humbling recognition of these centenarians who tend to live by the saying, "It takes a village to raise children."

As a side effect of their sustainable practices, the elderly are not socially isolated in their later years. They continue to live with purpose, they are naturally fit, of healthy weight, and highly active even in their 90s and 100s. The difference between this culture and ours is that they aren't so much *seeking* great health, but *enjoying* great health.

Of course, I realize not everyone can live with their parents or children. My family's version of staying connected involves one grandma who still works full-time and stays with us one night on the weekends, while another set of grandparents watch our kids a couple of days a week while we work. Prior to the COVID-19 precautions that we're currently dealing with, we tried to have all grandparents, aunt, nieces, nephews, and cousins over for dinner and a movie at least every other weekend.

Annahita Z. Van den Berghe

CHAPTER SIX

What Should You Eat?

Now, let's move on to the hottest topics in diet and wellness in an attempt to continue shaping and evolving your ideal eating practices.

Should You Eat Meat, and If So, How Much?

While experts haven't concurred on whether meat is ultimately beneficial or harmful to us, we do know that the people who demonstrate the greatest longevity eat very little meat, if any at all. It's important to note that these diets are best when they're comprised of whole foods, however.

We get into trouble on vegan and vegetarian diets when they turn into a "pantry diet." Even expensive, organic vegan pantry food items like veggie chips are poor choices even though they contain no meat. Ideal foods are single-ingredient and have the ability to spoil the way nature intended.

Dietician Dr. Gina Willett phrased it accurately when she termed these pantry food items as "pseudo foods." When they look exactly the same year after year, these pseudo-foods cause havoc on our gut microbiome, which inhibits your ability to maintain a healthy weight or attain adequate nutrition. Vegan and vegetarian diets are most valuable to your health when you mostly consume vegetables, legumes, fruits, nuts, and smaller portions of eggs or dairy, if you include those in your diet.

Referring back to our centenarian friends in the Blue Zone regions, they only eat meat (referring to any animal flesh) about five times per month, with portions the size of a deck of cards or an amount just enough to flavor their food. As author Dan Buettner explains, it is unclear whether the centenarians in the Blue Zone Diet lived longer from eating some amount of meat in their diet, or if they lived longer despite it due to the extensive amount of vegetables, fruits, and legumes they consumed. They ate some dairy, mostly from goat's milk, yogurt, and feta cheese. Most ate eggs two to four times per week, but no more than one egg in a serving.

Perhaps most importantly, people in these Blue Zone regions ate local, pasture-raised eggs from chickens that roamed and ate what chickens should naturally eat, as opposed to getting so plumped up with the same pseudo-foods we try to avoid. Chickens that are fed poor diets and become so heavy they're unable to move without experiencing fractures are what most people unknowingly consume. We should opt out of eating these for both health and ethical reasons.

Regions where people aren't highly attached to meat sources don't become affected by the productivity habits of large meat factories, which is where most of our trouble comes from. In other words, the meat that the Blue Zone individuals ate is very different than the meat the average American eats. Aside from the stress of the factory farm environments on the animals we ingest, the overcrowding causes the animals to acquire illnesses, viruses, and infections that they pass around to one another. This results in the use of large amounts of antibiotics preventatively and actively to treat infections. In fact, far more antibiotics are used than what's allowed in humans. Many of the animals in these factory farms die in their pens from intolerable conditions.

Pesticides are also commonly used to kill insects and bacteria, including the good bacteria we actually need for a healthy gut microbiome. These antibiotics and substances tend to concentrate in the meat, fat, milk, and eggs of these animals, which we then unwittingly consume. The meat producers often respond to the criticism of this process with remarks like, "People want everything cheaper and cheaper, and this is the only way we can provide that and keep up with the demands."

There's a better solution, of course: simply eat less meat and eggs, and invest in higher quality sources when eating animal products. By the way, it doesn't have to be more expensive to eat quality meat. One option is to find individuals who raise only a handful of organic, pasture and humanely raised animals, and buy in bulk up front for a longer supply stored in your freezer.

Fish is a unique meat source that has been accredited with longevity and anti-inflammatory benefits. I strongly recommend wild caught fish over farm-raised fish, however, as the latter often results in the same overcrowded pens, as well as antibiotics and pesticides. Food coloring is even added to farm-raised salmon to make it look like the robust red of wild-caught. Farmers say they color the meat because consumers wouldn't buy it if the fish was white or brown. Still, even farm-raised fish is superior for our health than red meat. This is borne out in general studies of longevity, so long as the fish isn't eaten in large enough quantities to cause mercury contamination.

Wild-caught salmon, sardines, and mackerel are great examples of fish that have excellent health benefits without high levels of mercury, which is a problem in some of the larger fish like swordfish.

To sum up this topic, eat meat sparingly at most, and opt for organic, humanely raised sources. There is much deceit in this industry with animal product suppliers using terms like "happy certified" and other words that mislead us into thinking we're buying/supporting a quality and humane product when they are, in fact, no different from the admittedly poor suppliers. Some will say "free range" but still stuff hundreds of chickens in a dark room where they can't budge from their spot. They just leave one door open to justify their label. You can avoid this by looking for the "humanely raised certification" stamp on your eggs and animal products.

As world renowned physician Dr. Tieraona Low Dog explained at a Deepak Chopra course I attended, whether we have strong opinions on animal cruelty issues or not, we all need to be aware of what we're putting into our bodies. She explained that the meat of an animal that has been stressed, is sick, or continuously treated for illnesses with medications simply won't be healthy for any of us to consume.

There are several documentaries, such as *What the Health*, that expose these companies that are mass producing meat irresponsibly for monetary gain. The book *Diet for a New America* by John Robbins exposes the fact that fast food chain restaurants buy the land in rainforests for raising cattle. This means the rainforests that are important for our air quality and where we discover new medicines have been destroyed by these companies at appalling speed. Not only are we opening the door to disease, but we're shutting the door to potential medical breakthroughs.

Prioritizing your spending toward your health is a great investment. Think about it this way: you either pay for it now or pay for it later with unpleasant and potentially life-threatening health consequences.

Again, while science isn't unanimous as to whether we should all be vegans, we do know that a plant-based diet should comprise the greater part of our daily consumption.

Vitamin and Mineral Deficiencies on a Vegan Diet

In my extensive research on veganism, I have learned that the essential vitamin B12 is hard to get through this diet. B12 comes from microorganisms/good bacteria that we used to have in our soil and water system. However, the use of pesticides and chlorinated water kills these vital bacteria, which has left us needing animals as the "middle man" to get larger amounts of B12. Animals eat dirt and insects, which gives them B12, so we get it through them when we eat animal products.

Vitamins and supplements are helpful, though they don't have the same impact as getting this vitamin through actual food. As Dr. Andrew Weil suggests in his recommendations for vegans, most are low or on the low side in B12 and will need to monitor it closely. There are B12 injections available that are often needed monthly and are more effective than taking oral supplements. It's also advisable to consult a dietician when on a vegan diet, as the combination of the food on your plate will make a difference in your ability to achieve complete proteins and proper iron absorption.

The vegetarian diet is rated far higher in the top ten of diets in the U.S. than the vegan diet. I grew up on a vegetarian diet from the start of my teenage years through the start of my college career. My father had been a lacto-ovo-vegetarian for twenty years and believed the diet had brought him success both physically and spiritually. While there can be a tendency to overdo eggs, cheese, dairy, milk, and processed foods, the vegetarian diet is ideal when we stay mostly plant-based and add a few eggs, yogurt, and dairy products in moderation—similar to the Blue Zone diet.

I recommend checking with your doctor to ensure adequate nutrition is achieved with your diet.

Studies show that vegans and vegetarians enjoy greater longevity than meat eaters by an average of ten years. They point out that vegans and vegetarians not only tend to live longer but are also more likely to stay married and physically active. Some question whether it's the lifestyle or the happier marriage and physical activity that add to their longevity. In this case, I believe there's an x-factor at work. When your mind, body, and spirit are aligned with your body's tendency to always work toward your highest health and highest self, you make decisions that support and manifest that will.

Then, that will drive you to healthy relationships, activities, and decisions that support wellness for yourself and others. Vegans and vegetarians tend to care about their own well-being and the well-being of others, animals, and our planet—a realization that people, animals, ecosystems, and the planet are all connected.

The Gut-Brain Connection

The Gut-Brain connection has been in the spotlight due to extensive research findings that reveal the impact of our gut microbiome on our general health. It affects everything from obesity to psychiatric and neurological disorders.

"Microbiome" refers to the vast army of microorganisms that exist in an environment such as our gut. These essential bacteria perform vital tasks that keep us alive, such as protect us against germs, aid in digestion, and aid in energy production.

The communication system from your gut to your brain is through the Vagus nerve. This gut-brain connection is so crucial that even if the Vagus nerve is severed, we have a backup system through what's called the enteric nervous system that continues the communication. While we don't yet know exactly what the standard (ideal) microbiome should look like, we do know that when the microbiome is disturbed through diet, chemicals like pesticides, certain medications (particularly antibiotics), and stress, there is a cascade of events that wreak havoc in the body.

The more damaging problem is when disruption of the microbiome, such as in a condition called "leaky gut," causes the protective gates to the brain to become more permeable. In essence, this means that the gateway that protects the brain from toxins is left open, allowing gut content to enter through the blood/brain barrier to the brain. Inflammation can occur in the hippocampus, a vulnerable area of the brain responsible for memory. There is growing evidence that there's a link between microbiome issues and neurological disorders such as Alzheimer's disease and Parkinson's disease, as well as psychiatric disorders like depression.

Have you noticed how many people suddenly believe they have Celiac disease and switch to eating gluten-free? This should interest you as only one percent of the population is said to have true Celiac disease. But indigestion and gut irritability is highly prevalent and very real these days. There is more evidence now to suggest that many individuals are suffering from a poor gut microbiome with all the mishandling of our foods, the chemicals in our containers, the cookware, the personal products, and even the chemicals in the ink of the receipts we're given at stores.

The good news is that we're also finding that when we change the gut microbiome to allow more healthy bacteria in our system, we achieve astounding healing and recovery. Interestingly, researchers have been performing experimental fecal transplants (since fecal matter is comprised mostly of bacteria), which has had profound effects in rats and in people with certain disorders such as obesity and depression. Researchers have found that transferring a thin rat's gut bacteria into an obese rat will cause the obese rat to lose weight and vice versa. They have also found that fecal transplants composed of healthy bacteria that are placed in a depressed individual improve the depressed person's mood and symptoms. The research is ongoing, but the progress and knowledge gained so far is invaluable to our overall health.

Threats to Your Gut Health

What are the biggest insults to our gut microbiome? The use of antibiotics is a major one. Sometimes, antibiotics are necessary because they save our lives, but at other times, they're over-requested. Some physicians feel obligated to prescribe them to avoid conflict with patients even when the antibiotics won't help. For example, doctors may suspect that the patient has a virus instead of a bacterial infection, and antibiotics can't kill viruses.

Also, as mentioned earlier, we unknowingly consume

antibiotics through the consumption of animal products. Pesticides, preservatives and emulsifiers in our foods, as well as certain prescription drugs, kill our good gut bacteria as well.

We can't discuss gut health without touching on the potential harm of lectins in our diets. If you're unfamiliar with lectins, they are naturally occurring proteins found in most plants. As a result of the recent rise in gastrointestinal issues, some sources have questioned if these lectins are toxic to us and should be eliminated from our diets entirely.

First, there is very little research to support that lectins are harmful to humans unless you munch on raw beans, which most of us would never consider doing. When prepared appropriately through cooking on high heat for at least thirty minutes, the lectins are mostly deactivated, and the beans are deemed more than safe. In fact, they're highly nutritious. These foods high in lectins are the most fibrous and nutritious available to us, including the foods we need for good gut health and maintaining a healthy weight.

In fact, for centuries, our healthiest people and healthiest diets have included a side of beans daily and many of the vegetables listed as high in lectins—without any side effects but longevity and wellness.

So why are there books suggesting that nightshade vegetables, legumes, and even nuts are toxic for us? This baffled me when I first heard about it, so I researched it extensively.

Perhaps we have to consider that we've strayed far from the natural state of our foods, soils, and environments with pesticides, toxic sprays, personal products, antibiotics, hormones, and genetically modified foods, all of which disrupt our microbiome and our ability to properly digest our food. Everything from our gut microbes to our ability to obtain our vital nutrition has been affected by the mishandling of our ecosystem and the toxic makeup of our personal products. And because of this, it's difficult to identify the definitive culprits in all the health issues that continue to arise in our society today.

So, is the problem with lectins in our diets or the possibility that our altered gut microbiome is now poorly equipped to *digest* the lectins? Here's an analogy: let's say I have a patient with a torn and inflamed rotator cuff tendon. He tells me, "When I stretch my arms overhead, I get this awful pain." Is the answer to tell him that stretching overhead is the culprit, that it's wrong and bad to stretch, and that it caused the rotator cuff tear and inflammation? Or is the underlying problem that his rotator cuff tendon is inflamed and having an abnormal response to the normally healthy activity of stretching overhead? I'm going to go with the latter on this one.

Similarly, when I hear of the plants and vegetables blamed for all of our health, gut, and digestion issues, I can't help but notice that our society hasn't been shown to have issues with overconsumption of any vegetables, including nightshades. A seminar I attended roughly six years ago on ideal diets discussed our highly deficient vegetable and fruit intake in the western diet. What further surprised me is they reported that the tomato (considered both a fruit and vegetable) was the number one vegetable eaten in the United States. However, this high consumption of tomatoes was from the ketchup we spread on our hamburgers and french fries. Do you see where I'm going with this? Americans have long been deficient in eating vegetables compared to the people in longevity regions who primarily eat vegetables and beans (all high in lectins).

In fact, our longest living Americans are Seventh Day Adventists who eat plant-based diets comprising of primarily all fruits, vegetables, and beans. Yet, they outlive the average American by ten years. Can you overdo it and have too many lectins in your diet? Sure, you can overdo anything and incur harm from that. The good news is that we don't see the average American walking around munching on nightshade vegetables, such as eggplant and peppers, as an uncontrollable habit.

I do, however, see a large number of us walking around munching on pseudo-foods from our pantries such as chips, cheese puffs, pretzels, cookies, etc. These food items are filled with preservatives and additives to add to their shelf life in the grocery stores and allow them to sit on our shelves looking perfect for years.

Unfortunately, the tomato is also part of the "dirty dozen list" of foods highest in toxic sprays and pesticides that further insult our gut microbiome. Now, consider the meat patty that's filled with antibiotics, hormones, and pesticides destabilizing our gut microbiome even further. Far beyond the lectins in the tomatoes, killing off the bacteria in our gut, which are essential to the digestion and energy production of all of our foods, leaves us without the capacity to process foods that have benefitted us for centuries. And those foods include glutens and lectins.

As a long-term solution, the answer is not to eliminate the most nutritious foods available to us. You may simply need to make adjustments in the interim if you feel you're truly sensitive to lectins. More importantly, you need to go after the underlying cause of your problem—the elimination of your gut-wrecking processes to restore a healthy gut microbiome. Then, you can more clearly assess if you have a lectin sensitivity or not.

A registered dietician is a great place to start. If you're found to have such a sensitivity, eliminating or minimizing lectins may be beneficial, but I think this is rare—even rarer than the one percent of our population who truly have the gluten sensitivity called Celiac disease.

Our longest living individuals in the Blue Zone regions have habits that maintain healthy soils, organic foods, and hormone-free and antibiotic-free meats and dairy. These healthy habits mean they have a minimal need for prescription medications. These habits collectively equate to a healthy gut that allows all pure, plant-based foods, including those high in lectins, to be consumed with only positive consequences.

CHAPTER SEVEN

Pregnancy

Pregnancy is truly a special moment in life that brings major and quick changes within the body. My recommendation to women who are planning to become pregnant is to first create optimal health and vitality within yourself before conceiving.

If you're currently experiencing back or neck pain, address your ailments and muscle imbalances before you become pregnant. Build as much muscle reserve as you can now, appreciating that everything from your muscle mass, balance, center of gravity, mobility, strength, and energy will change rapidly and will be greatly challenged. If your diet isn't ideal, establish healthier habits now. This will provide you and your baby with adequate nutrition; you will have the energy to create an ideal environment that your baby will thrive in.

Your baby will thank you for your preparedness, as well as your peaceful and confident energy state while caring for them inside your body. Keep in mind that babies are more attuned to our energy state than our exchange of words with them. When you're mentally, physically, and spiritually prepared for the major undertaking of creating a new life, the experience is far more joyous.

Once you're given the blessing of conceiving a child, consult with your obstetrician (OB) about what activity level is permissible for you. Most of the time, your OB will allow you to continue your regular activities as long as you don't have any complications. It's a great idea to continue with walks and other exercise, as it will help your body maintain as much muscle reserve as possible. The further you get into pregnancy, the more dramatically your center of gravity will change, resulting in a more rapid loss of abdominal and gluteal strength. But don't worry; you can and should return to physical therapy as soon as possible following the birth of your baby to work on regaining your core and gluteal strength safely.

Most pregnant patients come to see me when they start experiencing the effects of the protein hormone called "relaxin" further into their pregnancy. This hormone has many functions, but most pertinent is that it causes the softening and mobility that prepares the body for the birthing process. Women complain during this time of groin or hip pain when bearing weight to walk or stand up, as well as excessively tight muscles. Sometimes, patients tell me they have been stretching their hips deeply in the hopes of alleviating the pain, but they end up feeling worse. This is because the muscle tightness is secondary to underlying instability issues, so stretching won't rectify it.

The best course of action is to talk to your OB about a referral to a physical therapist who specializes in pregnancy patients, as well trying a sacroiliac belt to provide your lower back and hips with more stability. Manual techniques like trigger point release can also alleviate pain and tightness without stressing your hypermobile joints. These are far better strategies than deep stretching under these circumstances. Keep in mind, too, that you will be temporarily more prone to injuries due to this instability phase, and it may be necessary to adjust your activities to reduce your pain and allow more rest.

Once you have your baby, caring for them will result in a plethora of new discomforts due to nursing, lifting, and transporting your baby in a carrier. This is a great time to pick your therapist's brain on the best positions for using a pumping device, when nursing your baby, and when lifting your baby or carrier. Doing so will help you avoid neck, shoulder, and back pain.

Incontinence is another common occurrence. postpartum that many women are too bashful to discuss. Fortunately, there are plenty of options in physical therapy to overcome these complaints. There are therapists who exclusively treat women's health issues who can help you with the more severe injuries to the internal structures of the reproductive system.

To enhance the spiritual and mental experiences of the birthing process, embrace the physical changes that await you, and trust that they're supporting your wellness path. This topic is valuable because many women experience tremendous pressure to immediately return to exactly how they appeared before pregnancy. This is the case particularly with first-time mothers. I recall taking my size two dress with me to the hospital when going into labor with my firstborn. I fully believed that following the delivery of my baby, I would walk out of the hospital in my original size once again. After delivery, I humbly realized that wasn't going to be the case. These unrealistic expectations stem from how society convinces us that we all should be able to give birth, immediately fit into our pre-pregnancy jeans, and effortlessly return to work full-time after six to eight weeks. "And do make sure you pump every two hours because it's really important for your baby."

While it certainly can be done, we're rather nonchalant about this monumental birthing and rearing process post-pregnancy. Recognize that your recovery process following the birth of your baby will be unique to you. Spend your energy simply enjoying the moment, and understand that this chapter of your life may not be about looking like a fitness queen. If you judge yourself, you'll only rob yourself of what can be among your happiest moments and best experiences. Remember that change is both a positive and necessary part of the process.

First, commend yourself on the miracle that your body just performed in creating a new life and bringing that life form into our existence. In due time, your dedication to the health, rest, and nourishment of yourself and your baby will help you feel fit, agile, rested, peaceful, and aligned at home and work.

Pregnancy, Children, and Gut Health

There have been significant new findings about the benefits of breast milk and vaginal delivery in terms of the current and future health of your baby. During pregnancy and during delivery, the seeds are planted for the long-term potential of an ideal microbiome in a baby through adulthood.

Since mothers transfer their microbiome to their baby, it's also important for mothers to understand how to maintain a healthy gut during pregnancy with proper diet and avoidance of certain medications (if possible and safe to do so).

A baby born through C-section won't get the microbes that are most prevalent in the mother's vaginal flora, though they will get some bacteria that are more commonly found on our skin. Of course, vaginal delivery, while ideal, is not always an option. If your route must be a C-section, you may consider speaking to your physician about swabbing the baby's mouth, nose, and face with the mother's vaginal fluids/flora to ensure that this ideal bacterial seeding takes place at the time of birth. According to recent research, if they don't get these healthy bacteria during birth, they may never reach their full microbiome potential.

The advice on continuing to establish a healthy gut for our children involves allowing them to play in nature, touch dirt, and enjoy some healthy bacteria exposure whenever appropriate. In general, we all know the value of cleanliness. There is so much value in good hygiene and living in a clean and decluttered environment. Still, we were intended to be clean, not necessarily sterile.

That said, we may currently be in an era where the benefit of sanitizing may outweigh the risks in certain situations. With the COVID-19 pandemic and resulting extensive hand sanitizing, it will be interesting to see how this new ritual affects our microbiome. I put more effort into hand washing and only use hand sanitizers as backup when I'm unable to access soap and water. I try not to get restrictive about my kids playing outdoors in the grass, dirt, or with our beloved dogs in the vicinity of our home.

We appreciate the astounding research on the benefits of healthy amounts of sun exposure for adequate Vitamin D and have been more cautious with indoor public places during this time versus the outdoors. This era requires us to find a balance to meet our healthy microbial needs while keeping ourselves and others safe.

Annahita Z. Van den Berghe

CHAPTER EIGHT

Weight Loss

It's truly astounding that nearly two-thirds of Americans are overweight and/or obese, while many have the desire to lose weight and to be fit. There's a disconnect between our desire to be fit and healthy and the trajectory we're displaying with a steady rise in obesity, decade after decade. Why we have the desire to be lean is obvious. It's aligned with the original design of our bodies to function like an endurance athlete, as anthropology studies suggest. When we shed excess weight, it immediately feels "right" as we literally unload a burden from our shoulders. When we feel better, we're far better prepared to enjoy our life and partake of it more fully as we also become far less vulnerable to comorbidities.

Let's take a closer look at the path to healthy weight loss and the potential obstacles or pitfalls to avoid on the journey.

Step 1: There's an essential first step before any sustainable weight loss can occur. This imperative step is often swept under the carpet or unknown and not addressed: *to withdraw from our well-known and documented addiction to fats, sweets, and salt.*

I'm not making this addiction reference metaphorically. A seminar I attended years ago on longevity largely revolved around research experiments that found the same areas of our brain lighting up when we eat sweets, fats, and salt as when we use cocaine. It's no wonder, then, that we eat an entire family-sized bag of chips in one sitting. The product is created by purposeful design.

This seminar highlighted how the food industry is well aware of this addiction and adds fats, sugar, and salt to most of our foods (more so to processed foods). Even when we get a fat-free item in order to be more health-conscious, there will be an increase in the sugar and salt to make up for the missing taste of fat. Trying to lose weight without addressing our "sweet tooth" or snacking addiction is akin to being drunk and high every day while expecting to make sound choices about diet and portions. Health and compulsive eating cannot coexist. Once you wean off of this addiction, you can wisely use your discretion and discernment about when, where, and if these foods have a place in your diet.

While in the stage of weaning off sugar, salt, and fats (of course, I'm referring to overindulgence of unhealthy fats here), I strongly recommend not buying chips, desserts, cookies, etc. to store in your house. Doing so will set you up for failure.

When you do eat sweets, do so deliberately. Nothing is worse than eating a bag of something you thought was healthy like dried fruit, only to find it had sugar, salt, fat, and preservatives added to it (which you will find to be more common than not). Read the ingredient labels of everything you consume to ensure what you're eating "clean and pure" foods. When you feel it's time to eat a sweet, fatty, and/or salty food, you can then do so intentionally so that you stay aware of how much of these substances you consume.

Even better, make your desert/snack from scratch. It

will be your creation, which will eliminate the preservatives that are added to the store-bought ones. I've found countless ways to make banana bread, pancakes, and other dessert-type foods with ingredients that hardly change the taste, but make them so much healthier with good fats and fruit purées as sweeteners. The internet is full of these healthy alternative recipes for you to try. Then, you can enjoy these types of foods as a novelty when you're at a restaurant or someone's home for a meal. But it will make a big difference to remove them from your daily existence and reinforce them as celebratory foods enjoyed with others only intermittently.

In our household, my husband picks up a spinach queso dip alongside salsa and guacamole from our favorite Mexican restaurant about two times per month. While the queso and chips are thoroughly out of alignment with our diet, we enjoy them and look forward to the rare times we choose to have them. After having been away from these processed foods and tastes for a while now, I never seem to want to overeat them and get my "fill" of them.

This step 1 is the most logical place to start to ensure your long-term success and freedom from your "unknown" addictions.

Step 2: The second step toward sustainable weight loss is to raise your standards and make weight loss an endeavor of self-love rather than a search for self-acceptance. Your weight loss will be fulfilling and consistent when it contributes to your longevity, peace, health, inner beauty, and outer beauty. Many of us seek to lose weight in an attempt to look better physically, to feel desired, and to gain love from others. Too many people try to reach the unrealistic and non-sustainable body types of Hollywood icons—an arbitrary idea of beauty.

When you go to different countries, the standard of beauty is often very different from your own country. Even sixty to seventy years ago, U.S. standards of beauty were far different than what they are today. Unfortunately, for more than twenty years now, our definition of acceptable beauty has endorsed a body type so low in weight that it leaves us feeling unacceptable if we can't achieve it. But it's difficult for most people to achieve such a low weight because our bodies are dedicated to our survival. Being so thin isn't a path to ultimate health, inner beauty, or outer beauty.

Being underweight actually creates a dehancement of our physical appearance. The reason for this is that our body's vital nutrients will always be biased toward our survival in order to nourish our vital organs (such as the brain) first. Once our vital organs are supported adequately, the leftover nutrients are then directed to our less vital organs, such as skin and hair. Becoming undernourished results in brittle, thin hair, and the glow of our skin fades. Our energy level also diminishes, causing fatigue. In this state, we exude lack rather than vitality.

When I was eighteen or nineteen years old, I was measured at a mere 7 percent body fat in one of my KU health classes. To give you a reference as to how low that is, female athletes are between 14-20 percent body fat with essential fat at 10-12 percent. Regardless of the unhealthy category I was in, I was highly esteemed for my "fitness" and lean appearance, as it resembled what we idolize on TV. That reinforced my dedication to maintain my low weight. I was involved in a small amount of modeling, which further reinforced my behavior and belief that there's "no such thing as being too thin." But the truth is that I was malnourished without realizing it. My saving grace was that I ate a lot of vegetables and lean protein all day long to keep up with my marathon-level running routine, lifting of weights, and practice of Taekwondo. I had cut out fat (good and bad fats alike) altogether, however, which left me deprived and underweight.

That year, I went to visit my mother's side of the family in her native country. I hadn't seen them since I was very young. While I thought I looked fit and healthy, my grandmother gasped when she saw me. "Doesn't your mother feed you?!"

"Oh, no, Grandma, this is what fitness looks like in America. All the actors and actresses are very thin in America, and we all would like to look like them," I explained to her. Grandma didn't buy it, though she refrained from judgment and supported whatever made me comfortable. After a few weeks, I soon realized that people in her country were generally lower in weight than most people in the U.S. because they walked more than we do and ate fewer processed and convenience foods. They were mostly of normal weight, while my lean appearance wasn't considered attractive in their culture. Only impoverished people who had nothing to eat were as thin as I was.

It was the first time I realized that outward beauty and attractiveness are merely an opinion. One country thinks blondes are the most beautiful, while another considers a dark, exotic look to be far better. One believes skinny is beautiful, while another attributes plumpness to wealth and health.

That summer while visiting my family, I continued to make my grandmother cringe with my frivolous habits of taking four eggs and throwing away the yolks to eat only the fat-free whites. Indeed, in a country where kids were dying of starvation, I was consumed with my first world problem of keeping my fat intake to about zero. Only twenty-plus years later do I fully understand the seeds my grandma was trying to plant within me about life purpose and a healthy path. What I learned from her was to perhaps entertain eating one whole egg and add a slice of whole grain bread and fruit to satisfy my body's needs first. I could then donate three full eggs to make the day of a child or family who had nothing to eat. She tried to impress on me that what's best for me is also best for others. And what's best for others is also best for me. She was entirely correct.

Another profound experience I had at the Chopra Center in regard to inner beauty was meeting individuals who had truly immersed themselves in spirit, love, peace, and happiness. These people beamed with light and attractiveness. Yet, if I applied the facial symmetry ideals we've established as "true beauty" to them, I don't know that they would have scored perfection on that scale. Still, their attractiveness, smile, inner beauty, glow, and healthy appearance were second to none. No plastic surgery procedure, makeup, or weight loss technique will give you this authentic beauty that they effortlessly exuded.

Of course, not everyone at the seminar radiated this glow, as not everyone who attends a spiritual and personal growth seminar has achieved that level of self-love and peace. In fact, there was quite a contrast between the aforementioned people and those who fought and cursed at each other over seats in the front row when Deepak Chopra gave one of his lectures. It wasn't pretty (no pun intended). It was another reminder of how beauty comes from within.

Step 3: Refrain from becoming the guinea pig for every new diet that hits the market. Use caution and discernment before starting any new diet. We have become like a kid in a candy store swept away by every charming spokesperson promising shortcuts to looking and feeling perfect all the time without lifting a finger or improving our dietary choices. I have repeatedly seen this type of advertisement that attempts to make us feel bad about ourselves so that we're vulnerable to the sales pitch. One in particular I've seen pop up uninvitedly recently starts out with a young man with lot of energy who tells you to grab your stomach and feel how much fat you can grab. "How do you feel about that?" he asks. Then, he holds up two plates, one with a salad and one with what looks like a big bowl of pasta, sauce, and meat. He asks which one you think he eats and says, "I can assure you it's not this rabbit food."

I didn't watch the rest of this ad because I don't entrust my body to anyone who starts by drawing our attention to negativity. This marketing approach capitalizes on the common knowledge that people in the U.S. have more body fat than we would like, and many already feel bad about it. These are attempts to make us give our power and discretion away along with our credit card numbers. I know of no successful person who reached any goals through self-judgment, lack of self-esteem, or loss of power and discretion.

Your most powerful motivation comes with a deeper purpose than this. Losing weight with the goal of enjoying the gift of life fully is a far better driver than through self-judgment. Losing weight to optimize your life experience and watch your children and grandchildren grow up, while keeping up with those children and grandchildren, is a far more effective goal to take to heart.

No children? Perhaps the driver is to enjoy a more active lifestyle exploring the world, the nearby trails, or to be an advocate for a worthy cause. Maybe the weight loss is purely to wake up feeling good and enriched with the self-love to explore life.

When you see ads that try to victimize and manipulate you, laugh at how silly they are, and then turn them off. Switch your focus back to your true goal.

The next issue with so many half-baked diet plans is what I alluded to earlier about conflicting diet recommendations. Bouncing from diet to diet leaves your body confused and inefficient at weight loss. As we discussed how contradictory every diet and recommendation can be, think about the state of confusion that exists within your body when you jump from one extreme to another.

Perhaps the first diet you followed required eating every couple of hours because you were told it keeps your metabolism most efficient. Later, the recommendation was to intermittently fast for sixteen hours because it purportedly keeps insulin levels low, improves your metabolism, and results in weight loss. You scratch your head at the opposing advice, but you make the switch anyway, only to realize it isn't realistic to go without eating for sixteen hours on a regular basis. So you switch back to your old ways.

Then, maybe you hear about the vegan diet and decide to jump in without the education regarding pairing foods to get adequate nutrition. So you end up relying heavily on processed foods instead of learning to be a healthy vegan. Before you know it, you lose your adequate intake of protein and vital nutrients. This wreaks havoc on your gut microbiome, resulting in weight gain or loss of muscle mass.

In the next diet fad, you hear that cutting out carbs and eating as much fat and protein as you like is the answer.

If you feel overwhelmed, you should think of how your

body feels! It's as if you're trying to drive to California to hit the beach, but somehow, you compulsively take a detour that keeps landing you in Arkansas instead. Then, you wonder why you aren't even close to California yet.

When your body is in a constant state of "Dis-Ease," weight gain is inevitable, though that may end up being the least of your worries. A constant state of "dis-ease" eventually equates to "disease."

We falsely believe that we can trick our bodies into becoming fat-burning machines through unhealthy diet habits. The truth is that our bodies will outsmart anyone and any method, any day. We see this with medications as well. Whether it's diuretics trying to pull off unwanted fluids or antidepressants, etc., our organs eventually outsmart what the medication is trying to do. Then, we have to change the dose or switch to a new drug altogether. It becomes no different with these diet tactics. Your body will constantly try to regulate back to its naturally intended functions. When overextended one too many times, the wheels will pop off, so to speak.

Consider this: Let's say you have a one-of-a-kind, brand-new Ferrari, and I come to you and say, "Hey, I know how you can never worry about maintaining your car again. No more washing it, no more oil changes, no more routine maintenance! I've designed and patented this beautiful wall here. I will kindly take your car and crash it at full speed right into this exclusive wall that I created, and you'll never have to maintain your Ferrari again! Now, all I need is your credit card number, and we can get started right away."

You would look at me like I'm crazy. You would never hand over your keys because that car is far too valuable. But some of the shortcuts we take with our bodies are not much different from running our body right into a wall. Your body—your vehicle for life that's literally irreplaceable—should be given at least the same regard as a Ferrari. Instead of trying to trick your body or manipulate its natural processes for weight loss, try to support, nourish, and allow the weight loss to happen naturally.

Our planet and the natural state of our ecosystem have provided us with everything we need to give us the best odds for survival. You don't need to eat your fruits and vegetables through an adulterated tablet or powdered supplement from some diet plan. Vitamins and fortifications are intended to compliment an already healthy food-based diet, not to replace your food. This is the reason why vegans can take B12 supplements in doses that far exceed a daily allowance and still be very low or at the low-normal end of B12 levels when tested. It doesn't mean the supplements aren't helping, but they aren't helping to the extent they would if the vitamin were obtained directly from foods.

Am I implying there can never be advancements and a new healthy diet strategy again? No, of course not. People may come up with innovative ideas to expand on what we know now. The new data and findings have suddenly exploded as to the implications of our gut microbiome, with exciting advancements in weight loss, as well as the treatment and prevention of diseases of the gut and brain. However, most of these revelations have only reinforced and evolved from the truths we have already established about diet and health. The Mediterranean diet, the Flexitarian diet, the vegetarian diet, the Blue Zone diet, and the importance of a healthy gut microbiome implication all have a common thread to stay away from processed foods, eat naturally, eat less meat and animal products, etc.

These diets that get too artificial and oppose what has been established for centuries warrant reflection and investigation before we dive in. In fact, any diet plan that inspires you warrants a thorough discussion about its appropriateness for you with a dietician, your physician, or some other qualified healthcare provider. It would not be prudent to flippantly take the word of anyone on a matter that impacts your well-being without verifying that it's the right plan for you. And that includes any of my recommendations.

All you have to do is follow my directions, and you will never have to lift a finger. You'll lose weight immediately. Now, all I need is your credit card so that we can begin. *That was a test!* I can see that you're already learning how to become an informed consumer and diet critic who is immune to being conned!

Step 4: You knew this was coming—it's time to get moving! There are no shortcuts to weight loss, so you can't cut out this vital factor. If you aren't all that excited about physical activity, it's time to change your point of view. Once you start, you may find yourself hooked. Exercise can be addictive. The release of good hormones from physical activity, the feeling of accomplishment, and the tone it adds to your body all enhance your life. And it's even better with a partner and in nature.

One thing that will help is to begin dealing with some of the creature comforts you're accustomed to in your daily life. We're surrounded by so many things that flow from impressive technology, designed to keep us from even lifting a finger. I recently saw a house that had a pass cut through the garage so that they could pull in and put their groceries through an opening to avoid carrying them through the house. I love such clever ideas, but too many of these labor-saving inventions take away from our overall wellness by promoting a sedentary life. That's another way of saying laziness!

I see people flying past me on their bikes when I'm out trying to navigate big hills on my bike at my top speed. I look at them with amazement, and I'm inspired until I hear the sound of a motor and realize they're riding a hybrid electric bike. Now, if you're going on some lengthy bike adventure and would like to take a break with an electric version once in a while, I'm all for it. But if you're cycling for exercise or endurance, you have crossed the line from benefit to detriment.

When my husband and I were looking at houses a while back, we looked at a particular property that had shortcuts to the pantry. We also saw a house that required carrying groceries up two flights of stairs and across a long hall and living room just to get to the kitchen and pantry. This place also required walking a block to take the trash out to the curb and check the mail. Guess which one we chose? You guessed it—the "inconvenient" one. Avoiding creature comforts is a recognized contributor to health in Blue Zone regions. They live simpler lives with less technological advancements.

Of course, I like balance. There are certain tasks where I enjoy the help of technology. And there are other tasks I choose that encourage me to move throughout the day that I don't necessarily count as part of a planned daily workout. It's simply built-in bonus activity. I recommend this kind of proportion. If you're in a situation where your past has already taken you in the direction of poor health—things like sore knees and joints—you may not be able to opt for a house that requires you to ascend flights of stairs. You may be better off on one level. However, you can speak to a physical therapist or some other qualified healthcare provider for ideas about how to incorporate more physical activity into your daily routine.

Step 5: What does the ideal weight loss plan look like? Weight loss in its ideal form is closely linked to well-being, and the path to well-being is naturally inclusive of weight loss. Therefore, I recommend adding a sense of commitment and permanence to weight loss by viewing it more as a new lifestyle than a new diet. Over the years, I've accumulated many pearls of wisdom through medical seminars, personal studies, observations, and experiences.

1. The majority of our meals should consist of fresh vegetables, fruits, legumes (beans and lentils), and nuts in that order from the largest to smallest portions on your plate. Everything should be in its purest form. We will get to the frequency of foods when we discuss animal products, which can have a place in a healthy diet. But keep your plate colorful with various local—and ideally organic—vegetables. Frozen vegetables and fruits can actually have more retained nutritional content, as they are often frozen immediately versus losing nutrition while taking weeks to arrive at your local grocery (unless they're local). Of course, fresh local organic vegetables would be ideal.

Kale, broccoli, and spinach, in particular, are "superfoods" and highly beneficial. So they should be consumed regularly. Many people don't care for the taste of kale or spinach. In such cases, I recommend throwing these nutrient-dense leafy greens in daily smoothies alongside mixed berries, pomegranate seeds, mangos, and bananas. Add ground flaxseed, almond butter, organic or almond milk, and whip it all up in a blender as a part of a healthy breakfast or even as an "after workout" drink to re-hydrate and recover. You won't even taste the veggies, and your kids and/or spouse will soon be stealing your smoothies from you. I know—it happens in my home.

A fair amount of your protein should come from non-meat sources, such as quinoa, beans, or lentils. Quinoa is a great vegan option that's one of the rare plant-based complete proteins available. Most people think of quinoa as a grain, but it's actually a *seed* similar to a cereal and is sometimes used in place of rice. I like to cook my favorite vegetables with quinoa and fresh herbs in a rice cooker for at least forty minutes. I add olive oil, turmeric, and pepper for added anti-inflammatory benefits, not to mention great flavor. You can also add your favorite seasoning and healthy homemade sauces.

2. One highly controversial dietary topic is egg consumption. While the debate continues as to whether eggs ultimately offer more benefit than risk due to high cholesterol content, many dietitians advise that you not exceed seven yolks per week and, less if you're restricted further for other health reasons (e.g., diabetes). Each egg yolk contains 65 percent of our daily allowance of cholesterol, but we know our longest living individuals in Blue Zone regions eat two to four eggs per week, typically with one egg alongside a plant-based food such as whole grain bread (not alongside bacon and sausage!) Current research questions if it's truly the egg yolk that's connected to heart disease as opposed to what is served *alongside* the egg—the bacon, sausage, or other processed meats. And how the egg is prepared is a factor. If it's fried in butter versus being boiled or fried in a healthy fat such as olive oil, it also makes a big difference. The yolk contains the majority of the nutrition, and we know it can be healthy in small doses. I think for those of us scaling back heavily on meat, humanely raised organic eggs,

with no more than one eaten every other day, can be a great balance to obtaining some of our essential B12 nutrient, choline, vitamin D, and omega-3 fatty acids.

Here is a quote from the healthiestbest.com website about investing in organic and humanely produced eggs. It's from Marcy Dorsey, MS, RD, CD, an Evergreen Health Nutritionist. She says, "eggs from free-range or 'pastured' hens—those that forage for at least 20% of their food—have less cholesterol and saturated fat, more vitamin A, and three times the omega-3s, vitamin D, and vitamin E of conventional supermarket eggs from commercially-raised chickens. Eggs labeled "organic" come from free-range chickens that receive organic food and are not given hormones or antibiotics. The yolks in these eggs may be a deeper yellow and have a richer flavor. You will also pay a little more for them." Paying a little more is a small price for all the benefits of triple the nutrition from certain vitamins. We have a bias toward these types of eggs in my household, and the darker color and superior taste holds true in our experience.

3. All animal products should be consumed far less than plant-based whole foods. Yogurt is a great dairy product to choose. Organic yogurt (ideally, non-sweetened) is better digested by lactose-intolerant individuals because the live cultures aid in digestion. Some bacteria in the yogurt produce lactase, which aids in the digestion of lactose. Goat dairy products, now available at health food stores, are also far better handled by most lactose-intolerant people. Yogurt can help balance intestinal microbes while on antibiotics and can be very good for your immune system. On the back of each yogurt container at stores there is a list of the particular cultures or probiotics added to the

product. Ideally, you want to see at least six listed. The ones that have only one or two bacteria may not give you much in terms of adequate gut health. I love to add berries, banana slices, and granola to create an easy homemade yogurt parfait. There are some granolas now that are sweetened with dates, dried or pureed fruits, honey, or maple syrup that have some health benefits, but they still need to be enjoyed in moderation due to a similar effect on blood sugar as table sugar.

4. Consume good oils and fats, and cut out saturated fats. For centuries, olives and olive oil have been staples in healthy diets such as the Mediterranean diet and the Blue Zone diet. Dr. Andrew Weil, author of numerous wellness-related books, including, *Eating Well for Optimum Health*, recommends cooking with olive oil, as the amount of heat used isn't high enough to negatively impact the oil the way we once thought. There are other oils that are also heart-healthy, such as avocado, canola, sesame, and flaxseed oils. If you aren't allergic, nuts are also heart-healthy and packed with nutrients. I try and look for organic, roasted, and unsalted diverse nuts. Try a handful of nuts a day or a couple of tablespoons of nut butters. I look for ingredient lists to ensure that there are no other sugars or preservatives in my nut butters, as manufacturers often slip them in. Avocados are another superfood with heart-and brain-healthy fats. When my soup recipes call for butter, I substitute avocados without noticing any difference in taste.

5. Read the ingredient lists on any food you buy and consume! I cannot express the importance of this

enough. Companies invest a lot of money in misleading ads and food labels. Go straight to the ingredient list, because it's the only place that reveals the true quality of the food. Ignore labels that read "all natural" and "organic ingredients." It could have a list of twenty ingredients, but only one at the bottom is organic and somewhat healthy, while the remainder is unhealthy and filled with chemicals. The ingredient list goes in order from highest volume to lowest. You don't want to see undesirable ingredients such as sugar toward the top of the ingredient list. Once you become a professional food label analyzer, you will be shocked how many products sneak in sugar and other undesirable ingredients toward the top of the list. I have a hard time finding simple dried fruits when I'm baking, as most have sugar added. Eventually, I find quality, pure dried fruits, but it takes being observant to stay free of toxic additives that are frivolously added to our foods.

Ideally, the ingredient list is very short and doesn't list any element that you can't pronounce or identify. In general, we should opt for whole foods that contain just one ingredient. This will leave your pantry fairly bare. When your perishable food items far outweigh your pantry foods, it's a great sign you're eating healthy.

6. Embrace purity. Buy organic, humanely raised foods without pesticides, preservatives, and certainly not genetically modified. Avoid processed meats such as hot dogs, deli meats, sausages, and bacon. Support your local organic stores and suppliers. Organic foods should have roughly 25 percent more nutrients than non-organic. After saving money from reducing your purchase of meat, you can invest those funds in

higher quality organic plant-based food items. You will get the added benefit of taste! It's surprising to me how much better pure organic foods taste compared to the alternatives. If you can't buy all organic, there's a list called "The Dirty Dozen" that shows the produce with the highest amount of pesticides. With this information, you may be able to buy some of your food organic and avoid the more potentially toxic ones. We are essentially voting every time we shop at the grocery store and dictating what producers stock in our culture. If there's a greater shift of demand toward organic produce, more suppliers will have to switch to supply this demand. It's just basic economics. There will be more competition, and prices will inevitably go down.

It does ultimately cost more to not "cheat" with mass production and the use of chemicals, pesticides, and grain feeds versus natural feeds, raising animals in humane conditions. However, there is merit and benefit in helping an honest supplier continue to provide responsibly raised foods. This is a circumstance where "you get what you pay for"—and your health is well worth the investment.

7. Avoid snacking significantly before going to bed. A former patient of mine is an ear, nose, and throat physician (ENT). She explained to me that our bodies have far higher tasks in the realm of cellular function and clearing of toxins during sleep than when we're awake, and these efforts are hindered when our body must shift gears to digest food during sleep. She also explained the issues with indigestion and inner ear pathologies as consequences of late-night eating, over time. It can disrupt your sleep due to the digestion that has to take place while you're attempting to

> achieve deep sleep. Additionally, weight gain is more likely when we eat after dinner because you aren't working off those extra calories.

This topic relates to all of the recent hype regarding Intermittent Fasting (IF). There are spiritual and religious practices that incorporate fasting, not necessarily on a weekly basis but at certain times of the year. This is a time for inner reflection and spiritual enlightenment, and it serves a different purpose than how IF is used today. Intermittent Fasting has become popular as an approach to weight loss, but more so, it's linked to other health benefits. It typically blends sixteen hours of fasting with an eight-hour window of being able to eat. For example, you can eat between 7:00 a.m. and 3:00 p.m. Thereafter, you are only to drink water or no-calorie tea and coffee until the next morning at 7:00. The fasting days are typically two per week, although this can vary. The weight loss theory with IF is centered around the idea that sugar can't be stored in fat cells without insulin, and IF brings your insulin levels down, theoretically resulting in weight loss. The question remains, what happens in the long run if we ever return to our old ways? There is the consideration that we may be depriving the body and placing it in a "store as much fat as possible" state due to having spent so much time in starvation mode. Critics of IF say the long-term outcome with this type of eating routine could be slow metabolism leading to weight gain. Having fasted many times growing up with my father, I know that there is also a tendency to overeat once the fast is over because you're so hungry. It seems to me that the key when doing IF is to also maintain a Mediterranean or mostly plant-based diet, which will help you lose weight in and of itself.

While there are extensive benefits to intermittent fasting in the short run, we're unclear about the long-term impact. A nice intermediate approach (remember that

"Happy Middle" we spoke of?) until we iron all of this out may be to reduce all snacking after 7:00 p.m. The next eating would be breakfast when you wake up. This will be unlikely to leave your body feeling deprived or cause the anxiety that can happen with intermittent fasting plans or anytime you're on a strict eating schedule. Cutting out excessive after-dinner calories will eliminate the bad habit of getting nighttime munchies, allowing your body to work through its natural cycle of rest and repair.

8. How much protein do we need? Adequate protein is essential to achieving and maintaining weight loss and increasing lean muscle mass. The amount you need will vary and is related to your weight in lean mass. It isn't an exact science, as your body's needs may vary if you work out and exercise more than average, if you're recovering from an injury, or even based on your age. In the last few years of experience with dietitians, I've noticed they love doing calculations. They will take all of your unique factors to formulate a healthy goal. While that may be a good check on where you are to obtain a good baseline, it isn't necessary to continue constant calculations unless you have some significant change in your status such as switching to a job that's highly laborious or some other significant life-change. Ideally, these are guidelines you are establishing and customizing to ensure you're on the right track and effortlessly meeting nutritional needs, weight loss (if appropriate), and the maintenance of your achievements in the long run.

9. Give yourself a break and a pass ever so often. Enjoy a special occasion or an experience outside of your normal regimen without stressing over your choices. More important, let go of judgment

when you eat something you believe to be out of line with your goals at any time—even if it occurs frequently. Self-criticism isn't the path to success and will make the endeavor short-lived in contrast to allowing your taste buds and preferences to naturally adjust over time. Making a conscious decision to better your health is, in and of itself, an important breakthrough. The process of detoxing from years of bad habits isn't easy, and I commend you in your progress on your new path, regardless of how many times you revert back to your "old ways." Our bodies tend not to appreciate shocks and abrupt changes, so pace yourself. If you're consuming sugar daily, try cutting your portion in half or cutting back to every other day. It may initially feel difficult—or even impossible—to reduce some of these addictive foods heavy in the sweet, fatty, and salty categories. Just as some of us love whole milk, if we grew up drinking full fat milk, and detest the taste of skim milk or vice versa, our preferences are simply what we've grown accustomed to. Fortunately, our bodies adapt to any endeavor when we spend the time to establish a new normal. I used to tease my husband that almond milk was so inferior in taste to regular milk that I couldn't believe he didn't immediately spit it out. I refused to drink it.

Once I started a strict vegan diet, however, I had to eat my words and resort to almond milk exclusively. Surprisingly, I started to enjoy it. A year later, I transitioned out of strict veganism and decided to add dairy again. Interestingly, I now can't tolerate the taste of a cup of regular cow's milk and prefer the taste of almond milk! I could once eat an entire block of cheese in one sitting. Now, it tastes like a heavy pad of butter, something

I enjoy only in very small amounts. Meat tastes "gamey" to me, and I no longer prefer it. Although strict veganism wasn't a perfect match for me at that time, it helped me explore and learn countless plant-based recipes and to avoid heavily relying on cheese, yogurt, and eggs when I later returned to more of a Blue Zone diet and allowed some dairy and eggs.

Whatever discomfort you feel in your dietary changes today, you will unlikely experience this in six months to a year. When you return to trying sweets after a long period of abstaining from them, the high amounts of sugar will suddenly feel overpowering and not so enticing. Your discernment about what is "aligned" versus what is "noxious" for you will be more transparent without old addictive habits muddying the waters in your judgment.

I'll leave the topic of diet with a very profound Ayurvedic quote: "When diet is wrong, medicine is of no use; when diet is correct, medicine is of no need."

Indeed.

CHAPTER NINE

The Mind and Body Connection

The mind/body connection has fascinated me and engaged my studies since very early in my college career. While we don't talk about this phenomenon often enough in our medical training or with our doctors during wellness visits, it's a topic that deserves our consideration. One of my former physical therapy instructors—someone with a global reputation—gave a talk at a seminar called "Explain Pain." He told his audience to imagine a random man walking in a parking lot who suddenly sprains his ankle. Immediately, he limps and experiences severe pain, unable to put any weight on that foot. However, if at that moment, he were to look up and see a bus heading right at him at full speed, he would momentarily sense no pain at all and run on his sprained ankle in order to dodge the bus. How does this happen when we go from severe pain to no pain all in one instant? Our brain mutes the pain and allows us to move for our survival.

Another phenomenon is an area of pain that somehow becomes magnified or diminished depending on the news we receive or the perception of a desirable or undesirable event completely independent of the injury. A pain management physician I work with explained at a seminar that a patient's report of back pain is far different when they come into his office and tell him their beloved dog just passed away (their pain is often magnified) than if they tell him amazing news such as "I just won the lottery!"

What does this tell us about our ability to control pain? There's a physiological purpose for pain and inflammation that comes from an injury that facilitates the healing process. For one thing, it signals you stop what you're doing and allow your injury to heal. This response is necessary as a catalyst for an amazing process within your body to start healing the injury. Our minds have tremendous control over accelerating the healing process, as well as the ability to block the normal healing process of an injury through what is referred to as a "negative feedback loop." This results in an overactive nervous system. Therefore, more pain and more alarm signals go off than necessary.

These patients are often given a general diagnosis of chronic pain such as fibromyalgia or CRPS (Complex Regional Pain Syndrome). In these scenarios, there are no current or ongoing insults to identify causes of the debilitating pain. Therefore, treatment becomes difficult outside of regular pain management. The longer these patients continue searching for a cure, the more severe their symptoms become—even visibly—with swelling, discoloration, and various signs and symptoms of a person in severe pain. These patients often feel their pain is out of control, yet no one has an explanation for it.

They present with tremendous anxiety and often refrain from movement. This is where we confront the full circle of trouble in mind, body, and spirit. The anxiety and stress that something is very wrong and that no one has a cure becomes a catalyst for things such as lack of sleep, increased pain, and behaviors that aren't conducive to healing. Next comes the overprotection, inactivity, and lack of stimulation to that region of the body that opposes the innate needs of our joints and muscles to move in order to experience stimulation, circulation, joint lubrication, etc. Consequently, these people experience muscle atrophy, muscle tightness, and joint stiffness, creating an even broader scale of pain. The anxiety and fears heighten further symptoms. Finally, the obsessive energy and thought directed toward viewing that limb or affected area as a deteriorating part of the body reinforces this negative feedback loop. These three components create a self-fulfilling prophecy of deterioration. Ironically, patients are always in full control of dialing their pain up or down.

Consider the familiar term "placebo effect" when someone is helped by believing they received an intervention that cured them or improved their outcome, when, in fact, they were in the group that didn't actually receive any medication. Their *expectation* that they would be healed was responsible for the positive outcome.

On the flip side of that coin, there's a term called "nocebo effect," which is when a subject knows of the potential side effects of a trial drug and believes they were given that trial drug. They then report and demonstrate the negative side effects of that drug when, in fact, they were in the category that was given something with no capacity to cause the negative side effects they reported. What is interesting is these individuals don't just report the side effects, they objectively demonstrate them, despite not being given anything to explain their symptoms other than their belief that something harmful was given to them.

Due to this known phenomenon, some doctors have reported difficulty in knowing how to tell their patients about a small malignancy. Some patients have presented as declining in health—or have even died—from being told of a diagnosis that remained in its infancy even up to the point of the patient's death and was deemed incapable of being the actual cause of death. We have also seen the flipside where patients who are told they have only months to live due to a disease somehow overcome the diagnosis and live decades longer or may even be spontaneously cured.

While we can't fully explain these phenomena, it's imperative that we don't underestimate the power of our thoughts. We must manage our thinking to avoid a downward spiral of negative thoughts and emotions. While we can't confirm that everything can be cured by our thoughts and feelings, we have sufficient evidence that we make more strides by thinking positively and logically than by giving in to despair, hopelessness, and reclusive behaviors.

During a seminar I attended at the Deepak Chopra Center, a physician who believes strongly that the mind and body can't work separately described her debate with another physician who argued that there is no significant influence of the mind on the body. With great passion and animation, this doctor tried to convince the doctor of the connection by explaining all of the complicated neurological pathways that inarguably influence our body's ability to thrive or self-destruct. She told us how she concluded her summary of this debate with this closing statement: "If you still don't believe it, hand a teenage boy a *Playboy* magazine and then tell me there won't be a high likelihood and observable mind to body action and reaction that occurs from the mind dictating the body!" I think it was hard to argue with that point, and I imagine it was difficult not to laugh if you were a witness to this heated debate.

The most tangible way I can explain how our mind influences our outcomes is to remind you that behaviors that serve or harm us start in our mind and spirit. If we can put aside our fears and emotional attachments and work diligently toward desirable outcomes we would like to create, we can create a catalyst for behaviors that work toward our goals. That determination can cause us to be highly compliant in therapy. In return, that causes us to achieve results faster, taking our bodies to new heights. We start to gain even more confidence, becoming proud of our hard work. Our mind and body feel satisfied and empowered to carry out our new—healthier—lifestyle. When people feel good, they would like others to feel better, too. They may encourage a lifestyle change in friends who complain about similar back or neck problems that bother them or hinder their lifestyle.

Feelings are contagious. In contrast, think about someone who feels very pessimistic about their life, saying, "Nothing ever works out for me. I'm always going to hurt. Why am I wasting my time in this office and paying this copay? They don't care about me. I'm one of many. My genetics just aren't very good. All my relatives have this, and they didn't heal. Why would I?" Can you see what type of catalyst is created from this type of thought process?

If people have depressive or negative thoughts, they may not believe in the outcome enough to engage in behaviors that will serve them. They may skip sessions or dismiss their prescribed medications or home exercise program. Then time elapses since they started therapy, and they see no results. Further despair and progression of their pain may occur. The therapist may send them back to their doctor, concluding that they weren't successful with therapy, leaving the patient feeling lost. Unlike the alternative scenario above, these people are unlikely to be able to encourage others when they're unable to manage their own symptoms. They may even tell others to not bother trying because it just doesn't work. Unfortunately, these feelings are also contagious.

While no outcomes can be guaranteed in any circumstance, I can declare with confidence that the majority of my patients who came in with determination that they would heal, exhibited attitudes and behaviors that created their successful outcomes. I provided the tools for healing, and they ran with them. I have often said it isn't the diagnosis that makes therapy complex. It's the mindset of the individual receiving the care.

Let's Talk About Stress

The stress response was intended for human beings facing imminent danger. If you see a hungry-looking lion, for example, your heart rate increases to pump more blood to your limbs, you release hormones to prepare you for fight or flight, and your muscles tense up, preparing for potential action. These are just a few examples of the processes that happen within your body during stress. They are designed to help you run away from the lion or to try to fight it.

Of course, in our day, being pursued by lions isn't a main or likely source of stress. Instead, we experience it due to toxic relationships and work environments, as well as worries about money, health, our children, aging, and self-esteem, just to name a few. For many people, there seems to be no end to the stress response, one that has now morphed from something intended to save your life to a process that can make you very ill over time. Experiencing long-term stress can result in an increased heart rate and elevated blood pressure. This can cause your arteries to become sticky and put you at risk for a serious heart condition. Stress hormones change your mood and dietary habits, often resulting in weight gain. Stress causes gastrointestinal conditions such as diarrhea and can lead to

The Intellect of the Mind, Body, and Spirit

depression, which can lead to a sluggish gut.

Within the musculoskeletal system, stress can cause headaches, hypersensitivity, and general body aches in muscles that are tense due to stress. It can also lead to sleep loss, which triggers a whole other array of health challenges.

I have often joked that physical therapists are at times like the bartender who listens to the stories and stressors a patient chooses to share. It isn't unusual for patients to describe events going on in their lives and how hard it is to keep up with daily demands. They express that the pressure brings out sides of them they claim they don't even recognize. These are commonly individuals with big hearts who are selfless and have the desire to make others happy. Not all stressed individuals are "people-pleasers," of course, but there's a category of this personality type that, when unchecked, can become very destructive.

I love an analogy I heard during the Deepak Chopra course, "A Journey into Healing." Speaking on the topic of self-care, a physician said to think about what flight attendants always tell you before a plane takes off. In case of an emergency, an oxygen mask will drop down. Put your mask on first before assisting your children and others. "On a typical entertaining Southwest Airlines flight, the flight attendant facetiously followed those instructions with, 'if you have more than one child, then pick the child with the most potential to help next!'"

What do you think when you hear the instruction, "put your oxygen mask on first before helping others"? What happens if you can't breathe and are still trying to help others? For one thing, you become inadequate at it. Once you are further oxygen-deprived, you become more harmful than helpful.

In a real sense, people are living in a kind of depleted energy state each day, yet still trying to be there for others. What they fail to appreciate is that not taking care of yourself first can be the most selfish and destructive position to take for those you love and those you're trying to help. You also deserve to be included on the list of people you serve and think about. There are times when it's obvious that we need to think of another's needs before our own, such as during an emergency or while caring for a baby.

However, most people are not overextended from normal duties. It's the accumulation of countless other tasks. Identifying the life-sapping forces in your life and sometimes saying "no" to them is the healthiest thing you can do for yourself and your loved ones.

What I found to be most noteworthy during my training in stress management is the *Upsides to Stress* book written by psychologist Kelly McGonigal. In this book and during her lectures played on INR seminars continuing education, Kelly describes a rather lengthy study that found people who reported extensive stress and perceived the stress as bad for their health were far more likely to die from that stress than those who perceived their stress as something they could overcome. In other words, if you're going to have stress, at least don't stress about stressing!

Perceiving every situation as something you can handle, no matter how dire the circumstance, appears to have significant health benefits and may serve as protection from the potentially harmful physiological effects of stress.

Everything is Perception

Coming from a background that embraced exercise, workouts, and fitness challenges in addition to my training as a physical therapist, my perception of muscle soreness following a healthy workout was always highly positive. After all, I know this is the process our bodies go through to become stronger and better. In fact, when I work out and feel the muscle burn the next day, I'm more encouraged than ever that I made an objective difference through the demands I intentionally placed on my muscles. While I view an appropriate amount of muscle soreness after a workout as a normal part of the "growing pains" in the recovery process, I never allow activities in my clinic where my patients report their original pain and symptoms are reproduced. This is where I draw the line between progress toward our goals through a little healthy muscle burn/fatigue and aggravating the condition. One great example of this realization that "everything is perception" more than it's "good" or "bad" is a patient who was sent to me by one of my referring physicians. This physician had gravitated to my style of pushing patients to their healthiest limits and shared my vision of empowering patients to take their health into their own hands. The patient had driven a long distance to see me. She had great respect for this referring doctor and wanted to follow his recommendations about where to receive her therapy. With high hopes of the magic wand she thought I held to cure her debilitating knee pain, she gave me a history of her difficulties with standing up from her couch and toilet seat. She was in her mid-40s, with pain and swelling in both knees after simple tasks such as walking through the aisles in the grocery store.

After examining her, I found she hadn't worked out much and was grossly deconditioned throughout her core, buttocks, and legs. She confirmed my suspicions when she told me she was naturally thin and had never felt compelled to exercise much. Given her reports with difficulty in standing up and walking, we prudently worked up to functional exercises such as a miniature squat to start activating the invaluable gluteal muscles that would help her stand and walk. She felt no increase in pain in her knees, though she was fatigued after therapy.

"Wow," she said, with a tone of surprise. "This is a lot of work!"

To my surprise, during her next visit, she was distressed and upset about how sore her muscles felt the day after her therapy session. "I have never had so much pain in my life. It wasn't just knee pain anymore, but everything else hurt so badly I could barely stand up or walk. If it hadn't been for my doctor telling me what great results he gets with you for his patients, I would've never come back!" she told me candidly.

I immediately sensed she was somewhat scared that things were getting worse under my direction. This was the first time I realized that some people have never experienced muscle burn after a workout and, therefore, might not appreciate it as much as I do. I was simply happy that the symptoms in her knees hadn't returned. I knew the rest of her problems would work themselves out with practice and time. I carefully educated her about the "growing pains" that can occur when we initially begin to challenge our muscles.

Fortunately, she stuck with the program and worked diligently at home despite her fears. After a session or two, she began to experience less soreness and was even able to get challenged more at each session. Her spirits were clearly uplifted. She would tease me, "I'm so sore all over from your workouts that I don't even notice any knee pain anymore. Is your tactic of therapy that if you kick someone in the shins, they'll forget about the pain they came here for?"

I knew I'd gained her trust again and responded with a grin, "Would you like a little cheese with that whine? Let's double our sets today; that looks way too easy for you." My patient's fears were fading away, and she was seeing the positive because her original pain hadn't presented at all. Soon, even the muscle burns disappeared, and I had to work harder and harder to challenge her. She started feeling stronger and was excited she could stand up and walk from low surfaces without pain of any kind. She was pleasantly surprised when she noticed cosmetically appealing changes such as muscle tone and new definition in her legs and core. She thanked me sincerely for not giving up on her when she was initially so "crabby." I thanked her for all her hard work and for allowing me to be a part of her recovery process. She had met all her goals, and before long it was time for her to graduate from therapy.

Just as I was graduating that patient, I received a promotion to start and direct a new and bigger clinic. A few weeks later, my patient drove even farther just to stop by my new clinic to tell me how great it was to go on a trip to Las Vegas, with all the walking it entailed, without any pain or discomfort in her knees. She was excited as she explained to me, "I push myself to perform more reps and sets of my exercises because they have become too easy now. Plus, I just love the feeling of muscle soreness!" There was a big grin on my face when she made that last remark, and I told her how proud I was of her.

Many things in life are simply the way we view them. A very profound patient and tremendous entrepreneur once told me about a fascinating research article he had read comparing happy people with unhappy people. The research found that "happy people" didn't necessarily have happier circumstances or constant good luck in life, escaping hardships. In fact, the circumstances both the "happy group" and "unhappy group" dealt with were alike in degree. However, it was their *perception* of their circumstances and the meaning they applied to their life experiences that resulted in their description of themselves as "happy" or "unhappy."

It's similar to considering two siblings whose parents go through a divorce. The siblings are dealt the exact same cards. They have the same parents, the same set up, basically all the same circumstances, but you might find that one handles the experience of parental divorce in a reasonable and well-adjusted manner, while the other experiences fear, anger, lashing out, reckless behaviors, an attachment to how things once were, and fear about what the future will hold.

Many situations that arise are as horrible or as hopeful as we perceive and project them to be. Once again, the ball is fully in our court, whether we choose to be happy and view obstacles as opportunities for growth, or unhappy, seeing things as "over."

CHAPTER TEN

Mindfulness

Most of us accept the common knowledge that adopting a lifestyle that includes regular activity and a healthy diet is the key to preventing diseases such as a heart attack or even musculoskeletal injuries. We know that in order to prevent dental issues, we must brush our teeth. Still, it's rare to hear experts talk to us about the importance of prevention when it comes to our *spiritual* health.

Many of us wait until dire circumstances occur before turning to prayer, and that's mainly about fixing a difficult situation. Just as the path to wellness is far easier if we don't wait for a heart attack before paying attention to our physical health, the path to spiritual health involves spending time every day in reflection and *gratitude* before a crisis occurs. This practice of daily meditation, prayer, or mindfulness does for our spirit what reading and learning do for our brain, or what diet and exercise do for our physical health. In other words, it keeps the "bad" stuff from happening in the first place just as we see our healthy behaviors preventing physical diseases. Regular spiritual health practice creates a bond with our intuitive self in reference to the world, and it operates much like a guide or even a GPS, navigating us through life at our safest, happiest, and most optimal performance level as it leads us to our intended destination.

If you have tried meditation or mindfulness practice only sporadically, you may feel that it's ineffective. Just like any other skill, it takes time and practice in order to become proficient. It takes faith and commitment to your spiritual practice alongside a habit of reflection to effectively connect the dots and notice the changes that will inevitably come into your life. One of my patients once told me she believes "prayer is talking to God, while meditation is listening God." It's during these invaluable moments of silence and presence that you receive guidance on your next best step toward whatever you're asking for or praying about.

What is Mindfulness— and how do you add it into your daily life? It's the practice of becoming aware of how your body feels in reference to how everything feels around you in the external world. It's important to not judge your observations by labeling them as "good" or "bad," though a basic understanding of what's happening in the present moment within you and around you will provide guidance as to your best next step. This is because your body in its natural state is always moving you toward ideal health.

Most of us spend the better part of each day on autopilot, going through the motions. We're consumed with our routines and distracted by so many communication devices with little time to reflect on whether or not our daily habits are serving us well. We discussed mindfulness earlier in the context of your workout routine—the idea of consciously scanning your body before you pick the activity that you sense would most benefit you that day. One day, your body might feel excessively tight, drawing you to a yoga class or stretching. Another day, you may feel you have more energy than you can contain. You may even notice some anxiety. This could be a great day to do a longer cardiovascular exercise somewhere in nature, where you can become more grounded.

Mindfulness is also a very powerful tool for healthy eating and weight loss. If you have ever fallen into the trap of emotional binge eating, you know that it doesn't leave you feeling good afterward— physically or spiritually. It didn't fix the problem, and then, you felt guilty about what you ate. Especially when feeling emotional, you should take a few minutes to scan your body up and down and listen to the pace of your breathing. Notice any muscle tension, headaches, or gut aches. Again, it's vital that you perform this scan without judgment. Then, once your body relaxes, see if you can get a vision of what would feel most nourishing, and go with it.

With regard to what's happening around you—the external world—you may notice that you frequently run into circumstances in your daily life that don't feel quite "right." Let's use this analogy: every day, you encounter a large pothole on the way to work. And let's suppose you fall into that same pothole daily. It has become an accepted part of your journey. But perhaps this particular day, your mindfulness suggests there's a *different* path that will get you to work—one that doesn't require you to fall into a pothole.

When it comes to career enhancement, mindfulness may not only take you around the pothole (meaning, a strategy of dodging conflict at work), but it may take you to a completely different place of work—an opportunity that you didn't think was possible. One of my former employees had been with us for eleven years. During the last few years of her employment, I could see her growing bored, unhappy, and frustrated with the limited growth her position inherently offered. She didn't feel her job was fulfilling, and she mentioned her family and friends didn't respect her abilities or potential due to stagnation in the position.

From my perspective, she also frequently seemed to question her own abilities. The world is your mirror and reflects how you feel about yourself through others. She never made the jump to try anything different, instead accepting her comfort zone. She was complacent in our office for many years. During the COVID-19 lockdown, she was relieved from her position by the corporate office along with many others who were either furloughed or terminated. We always had a great working relationship, so she contacted me the minute she was let go to fill me in.

She was in tears, mortified, and full of anxiety about how she would support her family and find another job with pandemic-driven layoffs everywhere. I told her I was very sorry about what had happened, though I had a strong feeling this was the ammunition she needed long ago to finally evolve in her career.

Fast forward a few months later. She texted me with the exciting news that she was making more money—"a ton more money," she said—and loves her new job. She now manages a group of hero nurses who work through a crisis travel agency. She travels with these nurses and loves helping patients alongside them. She enjoys being more in the action seat versus on the sidelines. This position fits her personality much better than her former job. She admitted to me that she now realizes getting fired was a blessing in disguise.

Mindfulness can help you come to these conclusions much quicker.

I could have told her five years ago that it was time for her to grow and evolve, but I recognized she wasn't ready to see herself in the same light as I did. This is a caveat to mindfulness. You can't superimpose your observations about someone else's circumstances onto them. We all have to come to conclusions and enlightenment ourselves––consciously or subconsciously—in order to evolve and grow.

Mindfulness also means listening to your gut feelings on a subject you're unsure about. Perhaps there's a major life decision that needs to be made, and everything looks right. But you have an uneasy feeling about it. Everything looks dreamy on the surface, but something bothers you every time you think about it; it doesn't make sense. Deepak Chopra suggests listening to how your heart *feels* when you're making major life decisions. I have personally felt much feedback from my gut. I can't express how valuable this gift of intuition can be— if we slow down long enough to listen to it.

I have dodged many bullets in my life by listening to this inner voice. It presented as a physical strain in my gut when I nearly invited something into my life that wouldn't have served my highest purpose. I have also learned to not judge seemingly "bad" occurrences in my life because so far, all of those seemingly "bad" events have ultimately been revealed as blessings in disguise. It may take years to understand why an event happened and how it allowed you to grow and better align with who you are. With mindfulness, you allow the opportunities and options to flow, and you simply go with your intuition about which path to take next. You aren't necessarily being flighty in your decisions, but there can't be attachment to any path you take. You will fulfill your purpose through each route you effortlessly flow toward, and you will "know" when it's time to move on to the next experience. I always like to make a conscious decision to leave every situation better than I found it, and I try not to create more obligations than I desire.

Meditation

Regarding your spiritual health preventative practice, think of your body like your cell phone or your laptop running at top speed all day long. At some point, the battery will deplete and need to be recharged. Think of your body as going through the same process. Even our endless thoughts and actions all day long expend extensive energy. With adequate rest and meditation, you can start to work on reducing stress, take necessary action, or let go of what you can't control by not doing anything—and finding peace with that.

There is now compelling research on the benefits of meditation, yoga, and other therapeutic activities that ground us. Harvard studies have used MRIs of the participants' brains before and after eight weeks of meditation and mindfulness training. They found increased gray-matter density in the hippocampus of the brain—the part that's responsible for memory—as well as structures associated with compassion and self-awareness. They also saw reduced gray-matter in areas of the brain associated with stress and anxiety.

Meditation helps hinder early cognitive decline and is a natural remedy for pain management and headaches. You may prefer guided meditations, where someone either guides your thoughts or helps you to clear your thoughts and shift your attention back to your breath. There are countless sources available on the internet to try. I personally like the Oprah and Deepak Chopra meditation challenges that are intermittently offered when you sign up for a free account on the Chopra website, or access can be purchased at any time. If a formal meditation session doesn't work for you, simply quieting your mind during a thirty-minute daily walk—surrounded by nature, if possible—has been found to reduce stress, improve your gut and brain connection, and release good endorphins that relax your body.

There are countless other benefits gained from the simple act of walking. If you can't start with thirty minutes per day for designated meditative time, you can start with five minutes or less just to get the ball rolling. Then, work your way up to thirty minutes when possible. I like to meditate first thing in the morning. I usually find a place that's quiet or surrounded by nature. I start with expressing appreciation and gratitude for what's clearly working well around me. With a deep inhale and exhale, I release anything that may be troubling me, continuing to breathe until the anxiety is released. I then focus on my breathing, keeping my mind as clear as possible. Initially, it can be very hard to quiet a busy mind, but like everything else in life, practice will sharpen every skillset.

I typically come out of meditation wishing for the ability to help everyone feel as peaceful and clear as I do in that moment. I focus next on my intentions and creating the experiences I'm drawn to. I try to feel the actual emotion of experiencing what I wish to achieve. This can be anything unique to your career, relationship, attaining desired abundance, or the common desire for health, peace, and happiness.

Try to make this a judgment free moment. In the practice of meditation and spiritual wellness, judgment is considered from the ego versus the spirit. To achieve the full benefits of meditation and spiritual wellness, I recommend practicing the art of being unaltered by the good or bad judgments of others, and most importantly, refrain from judgment of yourself.

Just before her big break in Chicago, Oprah Winfrey resigned from her old job to head out for the opportunity of a lifetime on the way to becoming the icon she is today. Her boss made every attempt to discourage her from resigning, including an attempt to instill fear that her new position in Chicago would eat her alive. She was told she wouldn't last and would come crying back to him for her old job. Can you imagine how different Oprah Winfrey's life would be had she not followed her own inner voice independent of the opinions of others?

It can feel like an emotional rollercoaster when you get excited and feel worthy every time someone commends you but plummet every time someone condemns you. When that happens, you're giving away your power and placing your value and happiness in the hands of others. The practice of meditation and mindfulness take you away from your ego-based fears and needs. If you follow the path of self-pity, your ego continues to lead the way instead of maintain the knowledge that we're all a valuable part of a larger puzzle with our own unique purpose and talents. While the vehicle you use may change from time to time, your purpose and self-worth must be embraced before others will be drawn to your light.

CHAPTER ELEVEN

Abundance

Are spirituality and financial success inherently in conflict with each other? In other words, does the acquisition of wealth and abundance take away from our spiritual development? Is it "wrong" or immoral to have and make more and more money?

If you feel guilty about becoming wealthy, believing that the world is a battle between the "haves" and "have nots," consider Esther Hicks's analogy: similar to how your experience of great health and well-being doesn't take away another individual's ability to experience health and well-being, your wealth doesn't strip others of their wealth. In fact, the more you purchase and exchange the human energy of products and services, the more opportunities you create for others with your contribution to the economy.

Feeling too guilty to buy anything that sounds invigorating to your soul, such as a boat, a car, or even a plane will only choke your growth and diminish the abundance of others who would have been involved in those exchanges. Material objects are all part of the human experience. When we live our life purpose and are doing what we love, we can't help but excel at it and become affluent and abundant in mind, body, and spirit. This means that we can't escape abundance, gratitude, and consumer attention when we're in the flow.

So don't fight it—go with it. If you're an enlightened human being filled with love, generosity, and a life purpose meant to benefit humanity, I hope you become incredibly rich. Why? Power, wealth, and money are avenues through which you can positively influence others. Are you more likely to share your plate of food with someone else if you've eaten to the point of fullness and know there's another rather large meal coming soon or if you haven't eaten for days and unsure where your next meal will come from? More than likely, in the latter case, you would be hesitant to get past your immediate need for survival.

Once you step out of survival mode, any stage above that will likely allow you to detach from the need for money long enough to help others. If you have financial wealth, the big question with regard to spiritual growth becomes: what will you do with it? Financial guru Dave Ramsey proposes that all wealth is God's money—we are simply *stewards*, entrusted to manage it. This phrase adds responsibility to spending in context of divinity. Dave's essential teachings include routes to create comfort, avoid credit card traps/money schemes, and produce lasting wealth to allow an easy and stress-free transition into retirement. However, along with the goal of financial peace is an emphasis on the value of generosity in our financial plans.

At one of his Financial Peace seminars that I attended, Dave talked about a gentleman who had consulted with him for some time. This client was planning to take a large group of family members on an all-expenses paid tropical island vacation. Dave remarked "compared to his wealth, this $67K trip was like buying a biscuit to this guy. So I told him, yeah, go for it." From Dave's analysis of his wealth, he was fully capable and deserving of such a trip as an act of generosity to his family.

However, the next level of generosity that Dave talked about with this gentleman was that he went to a church and funded a project to buy impoverished children brand new bikes for Christmas. He paid for all of the bikes up front with cash, which added up to quite a large bill, even exceeding his large family trip. Again, this was like buying a biscuit to this guy compared to the wealth he had accumulated. How can that not be part of the highest spiritual expression to create an opportunity to vacation with your kids, their spouses, and grandkids, bringing everyone together with this generous gift of a family trip? After fulfilling yourself and your family, it has to feel wonderful to then further extend that generosity to the community by buying underprivileged children brand new bikes. The next step could be to extend his generosity throughout the country and perhaps the world. What an honor to connect with and uplift others with the blessing of "God's money," or the Universe's abundance (fill in the blank here in how you define Divinity) entrusted to you.

Another example of wealth working in harmony with our highest expression is someone who has effectively reached extraordinary personal goals and then chooses to take on a higher mission or role in helping others, our planet, or our future. One example of this type of leader is one of our most brilliant minds, who is also among the world's wealthiest individuals: Bill Gates. Journalist Jane Velez-Mitchell highlighted Bill Gates's "Future of Food" project in a CNN report regarding animal cruelty with this quote from him: "For every ten kilograms of grain we feed cattle, we get one kilogram of beef in return. The calorie kickback is just too low to feed a growing world population. Raising meat takes a great deal of land and water and has a substantial environmental impact. Put simply, there's no way to produce enough meat for nine billion people."

Annahita Z. Van den Berghe

The world population is expected to exceed nine billion by the year 2050. Without people like Bill Gates and advocates such as Jane Velez-Mitchell who wrote the article, many of us would never take the time to think about the story behind the excessive amount of meat on our plates and how that relates to the non-sustainability of our planet in our children's future as early as 2050.

Bill Gates is a good example of someone who has an inconceivable amount of wealth and intelligence and is concurrently demonstrating tremendous concern about the welfare of mankind and our planet. He is making a big impact toward reducing large factory farm animal cruelty by working on alternative meat options. How can using the vehicle of your fame and wealth to fund such a worthwhile cause not add to spiritual growth?

Can money cause corruption, too? There are certainly those who use their wealth to support corrupt causes, regress our welfare, hoard resources, and use their power to limit those of others. But if the money wasn't there, they would find another means of destruction. Similarly, those who wish to contribute to the world's collective growth will also find other ways to shine should money not be readily available. It isn't really the money itself that stunts or enhances spiritual growth. It's our intentions, beliefs about money, and how we use that money.

To recognize what you want your legacy to stand for in any moment is what determines whether you, your wealth, and your every impression/expression will be spiritual growth or spiritual regression.

I love this quote from Maya Angelou: "I've learned that people will forget what you said, people will forget what you did, but people will never forget how you made them feel." Emotion-filled intention and action are the most powerful catalysts to creating anything in life including wealth. A successful business/endeavor, successful marriage, healthy, and even happy and grounded children all start with good thoughts that create our words and actions to manifest that vision. That said, to acquire abundance more quickly, I advise that you visualize and write goals that go above the accumulation of green pieces of paper to what you would like to enjoy through that money. In other words, the money is just a vehicle—a means to an end.

A more purposeful example may be, "I would like to purchase a house in a great neighborhood for my kids to be part of an excellent school system." Or "I would like to accumulate the funds to allow a vacation with my family three times a year so that we can enjoy quality, re-laxed time together." Or "I would like to achieve financial independence to be well-prepared for retirement, remove debt from others, and enjoy the feeling of peace this affords me." I think you're getting the idea here. Money is merely a piece of worthless paper until we apply meaning and energy to it, which then fuels the creative process in achieving inconceivable wealth and desirable experiences.

How do some people seem to simply attract wealth, abundance, or anything they desire? It's as if they're just plain lucky all the time. This observation of how everything seems to work out for some people can be understood through a fundamental basis—the law of attraction. This is the idea that what you're attracted to is equivalently attracted to you, so long as you don't redirect your creative energy to repel the attraction with negative thoughts, unhealthy beliefs, or destructive cellular memories of your unpleasant past experiences (or those of others). The beliefs and positive feelings must be sustained no matter how long it takes to see the evidence of your wishes tangibly manifested. In other words, you must have a vision that sees through past or current circumstances to attract something bigger and better.

If you're spending all your energy noting all the ways that your dreams are impossible to accomplish, you'll have very little energy directed toward manifesting your higher vision. There is no need to burden your mind with micromanaging the exact route to your destination, however. There are infinite possibilities our human mind can't see in its limited capacity. Some of the highest and most impactful moments in life are spontaneous and completely unforeseen. This lends to the next important concept—to detach from the outcome of your desire.

Let me explain. Attachment comes from our ego mind, which believes we're somehow incomplete without that wish or desire fulfilled. Detachment with faith or knowing that we will receive what we ask for—or something even better—comes from a more profound and abundant spiritual reality.

From there, the resources and opportunities will simply present throughout your journey to achieve the abundance you desire, whether it's in the form of love, wealth, health, happiness, forgiveness—whatever abundance means to you.

Also, if someone else is fixated on your failing, don't worry that this will actually cause failure in your life. It will certainly bring lack into their own lives, as they spend their energy on you. But their ill will toward you can only manifest if you believe in that negative energy, which will add fuel to that negative fire. In that way, you co-create with the individual who wishes you ill. Make no mistake that you're in full control of your life experiences. No one has the capacity to take that from you—not your boss, fellow employees, family members, or negative or positive experiences. The gateway can only be opened and closed by you. That said, people either help you find your highest expressions or distract you from them. There is really no in between on this. It's best to spend the better part of your time and energy around those who lift you rather than those who "help" you question yourself and your abilities.

By the way, to achieve something truly meaningful in life, keep it between you and your internal source energy. One of my favorite writers and mentors, Wayne Dyer, said to tell others about our desires and aspirations may at times incite them to laugh, ridicule, or discount our creative powers and abilities. This has the potential to hurt our feelings and cause us to defend our abilities and desires, which switches us to acting on ego instead of from spirit or inspiration. Your wishes and ambitions are best achieved from within and on a "need to know basis" with others, at least initially.

There are those along your path who are essential to the process and to your success. You can share your vision with them. It will be clear and easy to distinguish those few individuals who are, in fact, aligned to help you. Of course, once you have accomplished your meaningful endeavor, share it with the world so that others can benefit from your brilliance, talents, and gifts. This is the fastest and most effortless route to your creative experiences and life purpose.

My Manifesting Journey

I'll take you through my journey in manifesting fulfillment in terms of abundance and career growth. One invaluable blessing in my life has been the experience of frequent contrast in many forms. I didn't always view the contrast as a blessing at the time, but now I see value in the perception and the resilience it has brought me. I love this quote by the Danish philosopher Soren Kierkegaard: "Life can only be understood backwards—but it must be lived forwards."

My start in life didn't include infinite monetary abundance, but my basic needs were well taken care of. I went to work the minute I turned sixteen and made it my priority to express my gratitude for having a job by going above and beyond in my work duties. When I bought my first car—which was actually far older than I was—it brought tears of joy because I had earned the money to buy it myself. My husband also reported a similar start in life, remembering his first car. It had so much rust that he could put his feet through the bottom of the floor and touch the ground. He nicknamed it his "Flintstones Car."

The beauty that these kinds of things bring comes from appreciation and joy as we progress in life, mold our desires, and attract more and greater blessings.

Somehow, the "lack of money" switch flipped as I continued to work in various settings such as the food industry, a sales department selling high line makeup and beauty products at the mall, and eventually in a hospital setting to get closer and closer to my area of study—all while I went to school. I had exceptional rapport with clients and customers, as well as the flexibility to work evenings and weekends. This resulted in frequent raises and *praises*. I loved bonding with my coworkers and succeeding as a group. I continued to feel grateful and took great pride in everything I did from cleaning tables to being a warm and welcoming host, or just being a helpful coworker. The energy that flowed from my appreciation and the enjoyment of intermingling with people attracted more blessings and abundance.

After graduating from Physical Therapy (P.T.) school, I

landed a job making 50 percent more in salary than the typical graduate. This momentum continued, as a few year later, I was offered the option of a partnership with a physical therapy group or the directorship of clinics that led me to spend the better part of my practice serving as a director of physical therapy for one of the nation's largest P.T. corporations. I took on new clinics—or old struggling clinics—and turned them into to successful, reputable, and profitable practices.

The biggest obstacles to success and abundance are our paralyzing fears. When I accepted the position of director, I was flown to the corporate office for training in administrative duties. It was a couple of days solely dedicated to learning how to market the practice. When I got there, I realized that I was one of only a handful of physical therapy directors/*owners*, while the rest of the group of about twenty-five individuals was exclusively made up of marketing representatives hired for various clinics around the country. They were charming, confident, and had a history of working in pharmaceutical sales or other marketing and schooling experiences. Those of us who were clinicians didn't have that kind of training.

I was at peace with the learning process of marketing until it was announced that the next day, we would be doing solo impromptu marketing "skits" in front of the entire group. In addition, the three corporate higher-ups would critique our performances, similar to what's seen on *American Idol*." When it was over, the whole group would vote on best marketer, and the winner would receive a gift card.

I immediately started hyperventilating. Standing up and talking in front of a group—let alone without significant rehearsal time—was my biggest fear and something I had intentionally avoided for a long time. I went back to my hotel room, stressed and anxious about what awaited me the next morning. I called my brother who made a great living from traveling and giving talks and speeches. He did this effortlessly in front of hundreds of people. I've always looked up to him, and I hoped he could help calm my nerves. He sensed my irrational fear, and when he couldn't talk me out of it, he said—with his typical sarcastic humor—"What are you so afraid of anyway? What's the worst that could happen? What—you're afraid you might wet your pants up there in front of everyone?"

While he said that to make me laugh at how silly my fears were, I instead got very quiet and eventually cried out, "Oh my Goodness! That thought hadn't even occurred to me! I'm going to wet my pants in front of everybody, aren't I??!" My brother then realized my fears were invincible, and his attempts to help me were only making them worse. He chuckled as he gave up and concluded, "I love you, Sis. You'll be fine. Why don't you go meditate tonight and just get it over with tomorrow?"

So, that's what I did. I resorted to a meditation designed to release my fears, and I surrendered to the process, accepting that there was no way out. The next morning, I was quiet, and my hands were sweaty as I watched each quick-witted marketer and director get up there, casually enjoying all eyes on them while they masterfully performed their skits. One of them, someone I had befriended, was the only one aware of my fear of public speaking. She consoled me and gave me a loving shove onto the stage when my name was called. I was the last performer.

I went up there and switched my mind to role-playing mode. It was as if I was literally walking into a doctor's office, and those watching me were merely workers at this pretend office. I felt a peace come over me, and I even started making jokes that made the group laugh. I was humble in my marketing approach, just as I would have been naturally. It was effective. In fact, when my time was up, I almost wanted to keep going. I was starting to have fun. I sat down and sighed with relief that at least it was over.

We were then asked to write down our votes for the best overall marketer.

First, you'll be very happy to know that I didn't wet my pants in front of the audience. Second, and to my shock, I won the vote—and the gift card— for the best overall marketing performance. From that point, I went on to be one of the company's top marketers, which contributed to significant referral increases and profit for the company.

After many years of successful marketing for various clinics, I decided it was time to step down from directorship over clinics to focus on taking care of my young children. I was asked to continue as part of their marketing team with any flexibility I needed. I did this for several years. Ironically, I was most fearful of what turned out to be one of my greatest gifts.

Just as anyone, I have many weaknesses—things that I may not as readily share in my books, of course. However, you'll never discover your true talent until you view your fears as merely opportunities to tease out your areas of giftedness. Many are crippled with fear as I was until I was cornered and couldn't wriggle my way free. I'm so glad that I was able to realize my potential because marketing ended up being something that came naturally to me. I love meeting new people, building relationships, learning from people, and hearing their stories.

I know you also have fears that limit you from taking a

first step. Fear of being laughed at. Fear of feeling inadequate. Successful people not only fail, but they fail *often*. One of the greatest hockey players of all time, Wayne Gretzky, was once criticized for taking too many shots and having plenty of misses alongside the goals he scored. He would respond to such criticism with the famous quote, "You miss 100 percent of the shots you *don't* take!" I love this logic. If I take a shot, I have a 50/50 chance of getting it in the goal. If I don't take the shot, I have a 100 percent chance of missing it. Profound. This is the logic behind successful and confident individuals. They don't count how many times they *miss*.

What happens when we put ourselves out there and realize our weaknesses? In my situation, remembering that we're all geniuses in certain areas and not in other areas, I knew that I needed to hire staff with the skillsets to balance the aspects of my practice where I didn't feel as strong. In this way, you don't need to be limited by your strengths, but to understand that you're valuable in ways that may be *complementary* to the skillset of others. This, then, co-creates your collective purpose.

Since many of our endeavors include some form of marketing or word of mouth, how do we become effective at it? Never sell any product or service that you don't wholeheartedly believe in. Set out to build relationships based on trust, reliability, and sincere enjoyment in connecting with others or helping others, versus simply "marketing." Your positive intentions and efforts have a way of breathing life into your endeavors in ways you might not think possible. I truly enjoyed the experience, the effortless success, and the abundance that followed me throughout my career.

Attachment

I'm now going to circle back around to our earlier discussion about attachments to our goals in this context. Once you realize that regardless of the circumstances of your past or current life, you can accumulate wealth and abundance, it's imperative to distinguish between *openness* to wealth and *attachment* to it. When our efforts come from inspiration, it's a different experience than when they come from an underlying fear about not having enough money. If your focus is on competition, desperate measures, and control or mistreatment of others along the way to achieve wealth, whatever you eventually create will come apart at the seams. When your foundation is toxic, a cancer will spread within your endeavor just as quickly as positive intentions would spread. When your empire falls, the self-worth you erroneously viewed through your money or success will fall as well.

Ironically, the mechanism for attracting money works best when we're detached from it and when we realize that, as with any other energy source, things ebb and flow. I was reminded of this during the initial COVID-19 lockdown, which resulted in my husband and me sitting around the house and twiddling our thumbs while work and life expenses continued. We were reminded about the transitory nature of wealth, as well as the importance of self-sustaining habits. Rather than focus on the loss or go down a negative fear spiral, I changed my focus to realize that I love to write as much as I love to read, and I was given a golden opportunity—to write this book.

I realized that I could touch lives even when not physically about to lay my hands on my patients. My family and I started to appreciate the simple things in life, and we let go of many of the frills that we really didn't need in our lives. It was truly a time for appreciating all the aspects of life that are so valuable and cost nothing—such as uninterrupted family time. When the initial lockdown was over, we had new appreciation for the fact that no one is untouchable and that we are capable of losing everything——a humbling, yet important realization.

One humbling moment involved one of our kids who started his journey in life with an extended stay at a neonatal intensive care unit (NICU), resulting in millions of dollars' worth of medical bills. Little did we know that the responsible party in the insurance system, someone who had been appointed to add my son to our plan, had been in the middle of resigning and had essentially "checked out" before adding him on to our policy. When we found out about this negligence and oversight millions of dollars later, our insurance company took advantage of the opportunity to tell us they would only add our son with a ten-million-dollar deductible. The rest of our kids were free in accordance with the original terms of the plan.

I thought it was completely criminal. I felt hurt, angry, fearful, and sad to have to deal with such an injustice during an already difficult time. I began to picture us having to sell everything we owned and move into a trailer with six kids in order to pay off this debt. Shortly after these initial feelings flowed through me, I redirected my thoughts to the realization that I had been equally happy in my life when I had very little. I remembered growing up in a tiny student housing apartment and many other humbling places while my parents were the stereotypical young and "broke" students. All I noticed as a child was that one apartment complex we lived in had a swimming pool that I would run to at full speed with my best friend. We would cannonball into the water with laughter and pure joy. I remembered another apartment complex that offered free doughnuts on Sunday mornings that were so delicious. I remembered the camping trips we took and how we roasted marshmallows. Further down memory lane, I remembered being a *minimalist* student early in my college career, yet enjoying some of the most wonderful, fun, and unassuming times in my life—and requiring very little money.

I recall the first time I became aware of lack. It was when I was in my first serious relationship while in physical therapy school and moving into an apartment with only a *futon* as a bed/couch and a few pictures to put on the wall. I heard there had been a robbery in the apartment complex and started expressing concern about "what if the burglar breaks into my apartment and takes all my stuff while I'm in classes?" My significant other at that time, who came from a very well-to-do family, replied "Are you kidding? If I were a robber and took the time to break into your apartment, I would be pissed! You literally have nothing."

It was the first time I realized as an adult that to some people, I may not have had very much or been very abundant. Yet, it had never occurred to me before and, therefore, had never affected my personal sense of happiness.

Bouncing back from those memories to that moment in time with my son in the hospital and millions of dollars hanging over our heads, I suddenly appreciated that while accumulating assets was fun and enjoyable, the beauty of experiencing opposite extremes of wealth is the realization that happiness doesn't depend on large amounts of money. And if you created wealth before, you could create it again. I also had an appreciation for marrying someone who, even if we had to downsize to live in a small box, I would still feel like the luckiest bride in the world.

As long as our family was healthy and together, the rest of it seemed rather trivial. These realizations caused a detachment in my heart and a detachment from the need for money, as well as an empowerment within myself that everything will ultimately be fine no matter what.

Interestingly, the moment I switched to this mindset and let my concerns and stress go, everything worked itself out. Suddenly, the hospital system realized that my son qualified for all sorts of assistance we didn't know existed. The end result was that various avenues of support started flowing to us out of nowhere, providing opportunities for my son even above and beyond his basic care. He was provided with complimentary haircuts, daily baby massages from a massage therapist, music therapy from a music therapist, book-reading buddies, baby-rockers, and all sorts of therapy and gifts. I teared up as I reflected on all of this at the time. And I still do to this day.

Had I placed my power, happiness, and future in the hands of an insurance company, I would have come up short. Their only generosity was reducing his upfront deductible from ten-million-dollars to six-million-dollars a year. The abundance of the universe, however, took care of my son, his hospital stay, and further meaningful gifts and talented helpers. I didn't put out a news blast about our challenges to suddenly receive financial support. I didn't squabble endlessly with the insurance company in an attempt to make them change their position. I simply let go of the struggle and held onto the belief that the answers and support would come in some manner I couldn't readily observe. Once you choose to allow abundance into your vortex, you realize that what brings you ultimate long-lasting wealth is your *creative energy* reflecting your life purpose in its most authentic way. It involves transparency, love, and a mission to not just do well, but to truly do *good*.

Annahita Z. Van den Berghe

CHAPTER TWELVE

We Are All One

No event in my lifetime has made the interconnection among us across the globe more vivid than the current COVID-19 pandemic. What starts in any one region of the world affects all of us regardless of our proximity or the distance to that region. This shows the potential for chain reactions that exist through us. Despite our attempts to historically separate ourselves in terms of demographics, race, financial status, gender, age, religion, or politics, we must humbly realize how alike, equally vulnerable, and interdependent we are during such trying moments. There is a clear dividing of the prism for those who seek to help vulnerable or high-risk individuals versus those who cause chaos and fight with overextended employees at the grocery store in order to hoard limited items.

For many people, this has been a time of reflection—an enlightening moment when our leaders need cooperation, transparency, knowledge, and insight from all of us to overcome a pandemic that impacts everyone regardless of race, religion, nationality, financial status, or power. The only true immunity is our ability to ground ourselves, think logically, and lift each other up. We are realizing that wishing wellness in Wuhan or any and every other country in the world is essentially wishing wellness for ourselves. The healthier we are around the globe, the healthier we are here at home.

Annahita Z. Van den Berghe

When I was a teenager, I had a traditional Korean Taekwondo instructor who used to spend just as much time building our character, ethics, and morals as he did teaching us self-defense techniques. At the end of each class, in his broken English, he would read portions of the Bible to us or Chinese Proverbs. I was only thirteen years old when I heard this one proverb, in particular, that seems so perfect in describing what I believe is not only our way out of this "crisis," but a way to make us even stronger and more united than we were before. Grand Master Ki June Park read us a story that went something like this, as I recall: A man asked to see what Heaven and Hell are truly like. His wish was granted as he was taken to view what he wished to see and understand. They first went to visit what we have labeled as "Heaven." As the golden gates opened, the man's eyes grew bigger and bigger in excitement and anticipation. There were heavenly angels playing music, singing, and dancing. The beautiful, colorful birds were singing in perfect harmony. There were decorations of gold and shining diamonds as far as the eyes could see. The rivers were flowing with refreshing water, and the most amazing smells of food this man had ever experienced filled the air. There was a circle of bright individuals glowing with light and love sitting joyfully together. What was odd was that each being of light had an excessively long six-foot spoon connected to their hand that they were unable to coordinate to their own mouths to eat the delicious food presented to them on the spoon. Instead, they started feeding each other as they quickly realized, 'I clearly cannot feed myself right now, though I can help my neighbor who's struggling with the same problem.' This action was then repeated by all of them, which in essence, resolved the dilemma of not being able to eat. This action created more love, unity, trust, and gratitude as they fed each other the most amazing food anyone could have experienced.

"Heaven is truly amazing as I expected," this man thought. Next, he wanted to view what we have referred to as 'Hell or where fallen individuals are said to be sent.' The man was scared about what he would see upon entering those gates in contrast to those in Heaven. However, upon entering, he was quite perplexed to see the exact same entrance as Heaven. The golden gates, the beautiful river, the angels and birds singing, and the smell of amazing foods were all the same. There was again a circle of beings with the same six-foot spoons attached to their hands with delightful food on their spoons. In contrast to Heaven, however, the beings looked sickly, starved, angry, and frustrated as they obsessively attempted to feed themselves and failed because the spoons didn't allow them to reach their own mouths. The thought of feeding one another never seemed to occur to them. If they couldn't eat, then no one else would either. Starvation and deprivation were preferable over any one person starting the selfless act of feeding another, which would eventually squash the minor dilemma standing in their way of pure bliss.

This story was truly fascinating to me because many of us think about a time after life where we may encounter "Heaven" or "Hell." But I hadn't given much thought about the magnitude of what we're capable of creating in the present moment. Regardless of our cultural or religious beliefs about Heaven and Hell, this story is a reminder that we're capable of creating our own "Heaven" or "Hell" right here on Earth. We can choose to lift each other up, encourage, inspire, and pull through as one big loving unit, or we can split off, fight, and struggle individually.

Sometimes, it's hard to live out this type of heavenly love in serving others when it isn't overtly reciprocated. We haven't yet reached a collective consciousness (the dominating belief system or the sum of the collective thoughts in our world as a whole) that allows us to trust one another and exist together in perfect harmony. We have lost sight of the truth that we are all One.

How did we come to define ourselves as *separate*? It has mainly stemmed from the premise that we're different in terms of religion, race, or nationality. However, are we really all that different? There have been extensive studies done on how people living in various regions across the globe differ from one another in their daily routines. People in these various regions were studied and compared in order to see how different we are globally from one another considering our varying cultures and religions. The conclusion of the studies was that no matter how different we view ourselves in each country, including our politics and religious beliefs, people live very *similar lives* and *routines* around the world.

We all value and express concern over the same topics of marriage, children, work, general worries, fears, self-acceptance, etc. We have a comparable number of altruistic individuals versus less "enlightened." There was even a finding that people live longer, healthier, and happier lives if they're faithful and wake up with a purpose and a sense of something bigger than themselves. The particular religious denomination didn't make a difference, however. *All* faith-based individuals enjoyed those benefits, alike. There really were no fundamental differences despite how we view ourselves. This illusion of difference and separation brings fear of one another, locally or globally.

Generally, people living in any one country don't spend frequent time thinking about their hatred and ill will toward another country. The leaders of each country may or may not have some of these feelings and intentions, but the general population does not. They mainly get caught up in political warfare that's out of their hands.

I have a couple of personal stories to share about my family history that seem to fall in accordance with these research findings. To back up a little, my parents came to the U.S. from Iran back in the early 70s when the Shah (King) was still the leader of the country. Relations between Iran and the U.S.A. were great at that time, and consequently, my dad was able to get a full-ride scholarship to Kansas University to continue his graduate studies in physics and engineering. This resulted in my being born and raised in the U.S., though having some knowledge of what life was like in Iran following the Iranian revolution.

When the Islamic government overthrew the Shah in 1979, Iran was no longer an ally of the U.S. While the majority of my family left Iran after that event, my mother's immediate family was never able to find "an out," so they remained in Iran.

Outside of a couple of visits when I was too young to remember, we didn't return to Iran until I was a young adult. My older brother and I—at the ages of eighteen and twenty-two—decided to visit and reconnect with my mom's side of the family, relatives we hadn't seen since we were very young. I'll admit, I was rather intimidated by everything they showed of Iran on the news. Regardless of assurances from my family in Iran, I thought I would see all sorts of extremists ready to throw me in jail for not wearing my hijab correctly, or they would hear my broken Farsi (the Persian language spoken in Iran) and give me trouble.

When my brother and I first got off the plane, our fears and concerns melted away as we walked toward a crowd of people outside the airport doors. I looked at my brother in disbelief as they all started cheering when we approached. "Wow, is this how the people of Iran greet visitors? I don't even know these people, and they're roaring with delight at our arrival. Well, this isn't so bad," I thought, grinning from ear to ear.

All of a sudden, my brother tapped me on the shoulder and told me to turn around. The Iranian soccer team was walking right behind us. They were the ones who had the crowd roaring in delight and admiration. My brother and I couldn't stop laughing at ourselves until we saw our grandmother's face outside the door. Her eyes filled with tears when she saw us.

The welcome from my grandparents, aunts, and cousins felt a million times more heightened in my heart than any love that soccer team could've received. As I alluded to earlier, I had a lot of irrational fears from watching the news in the United States regarding what Iran was like and how much of an enemy they were to us. After my cousins hugged and welcomed me, they laughed uncontrollably about the "double hijab covering my every hair and inch of skin." They, on the other hand, looked so chic and European with their fashionable knee-length overcoats and sheer, colorful scarves. To my surprise, their scarves only covered the very top of their heads, allowing their long, beautiful hair to graze their waistlines. They had the most beautiful makeup, jewelry, and designer sunglasses and purses. They teased me, "Is that your blanket you used to cover your hair? I think you missed a strand!" I started to loosen up as I took the good-natured jabs from my cousins and immediately knew we would be great friends because I could dish it out just as well. I also realized that the media had painted a drastically different picture from the norm in Iran. I soon discovered that this culture I thought was so serious and Islamic could party many Americans under the table.

Alcohol wasn't necessary to help these people cut loose

at a party. They danced all night, laughed, and ate until the wee hours of the morning. Interestingly, partying was not reserved for the young. Folks our parents' age could dance circles around the young ones. To my cousins' amusement, I was one of the few people sitting in a corner still wearing my hijab at these parties or weddings. In my defense, there were a few grandmas there who were also still wearing their hijabs. Parties, regardless of how innocent, weren't legal when they were coed. I was only going to be in Iran a short time and didn't feel the need to risk time in jail when I barely spoke or understood Farsi (and didn't read or write it at all). But my observation was that Iranians weren't the Islamic stereotypes they were shown to be on TV, just waiting to set the American flag on fire. They were fun-loving people who enjoyed doing the same things we do and only wished they had a fraction of our freedoms.

As for my worries about my broken Farsi with a perfect Kansas accent, two things happened when I opened my mouth and spoke Farsi in public. First, my uncle jokingly begged me to keep my mouth shut, as prices of products would suddenly increase, as the negotiation game wouldn't work when they realized I was a visitor. Regardless, we're talking about kid toys costing one dollar versus fifty cents, so no worries about that on my end. But my uncle saw this as competition, and he didn't like losing the negotiation game at the markets.

The second thing that happened when my American accent got noticed in public was that people gave me the warmest smile and asked, "Are you a visitor? Where are you coming from? Are you having a good time? What is it like there? We wish so much we could leave here and visit America. Please tell them we aren't what they portray us to be. We love Americans. We would invite anyone to our house for dinner and take very good care of them. This government of ours keeps us as prisoners. We don't want to be associated with them. Please tell them in America that we aren't like them."

This was something I heard frequently from people in Iran. One middle-aged man with a big smile followed those comments with, "Also, please tell Bill Clinton I said hello!" I jokingly replied, "I will call President Clinton immediately and tell him you said hello," as if the President's number was on my speed dial.

In that moment, I realized that there's a big distinction between the intentions and thought processes of any country or government and the average person in a country. I wondered why other countries are made to look so bad. I mean, it would be like if you took a video of some out-of-control riot in America with people setting everything on fire or killing each other and that was all that was played about us on the news around the world. People would think that was our essence when it was just a subgroup of people during a turbulent moment, and quite the contrast from the nature of most Americans on a day-to-day basis.

My 23-year-old cousin in Iran was just a typical "kid" like we see here in the U.S. He loves to hang out with his friends and family. He works out a lot and enjoys tanning by the beach. He was blessed with good looks and earned an engineering degree.

He loved the attention of girls just as most young men do at that age. The only aspect more "average" about him than most in his age group was that he was raised in a family where charity work, feeding the hungry, and helping the impoverished was a weekly routine. To this date, his family prepares amazing meals, places them in lunch boxes, and delivers them to an area of town with families (even young children) living in cardboard boxes. I love seeing the videos of these homeless people in shock and tears at his kindness. They bless him and tell him, "Thank you, young one. I hope God gives you ten-fold, no, a hundred-fold in return for your good deeds. God Bless you." My cousin humbly replies *"Noosheh Jahn,"* which translates to "may it nourish your soul," as he releases their grasp to hand a lunchbox to the next person.

This sweet, typical "kid" was drafted into the army, which is normal in Iran, to guard the borders during the Isis crisis a couple of years ago. Now, the soldiers on the other side of the battle have likely been brainwashed with news about the evils of the other side—in this case my cousin. They have likely dehumanized his character to make sure they feel no guilt when fighting to him to the death. In reality, my cousin was in tears before this involuntary duty, wondering if he was ever going to see his family or his fiancé again. He also wondered how he was supposed to kill another when his heart is clearly pro-life.

Fortunately, outside of time away from his loved ones and the torture of having to sleep standing up and with one eye open for some time, Isis attack attempts during his service were contained before anyone had to shoot or be shot in his region. His education also gave him rank that made his service time far shorter than what it otherwise would have been. We were all very grateful when he was back home alive—especially my aunt. When our kids or loved ones are in the service, the prayers that they will reunite with us without serious physical or psychological repercussions is shared alike, regardless of what side of the war or globe we happen to exist on.

I'd like to share a couple of miraculous true events in our American and world history that gave me goosebumps when I learned about them. One of them was an

Annahita Z. Van den Berghe

inconceivable moment during the 1914 Christmas truce in World War I, when British and German soldiers came out of their trenches, abandoned their weapons, and yelled out "Merry Christmas" to their enemies. Fears that this truce gesture was a trick was trumped by the genuine Christmas spirit inspiring faith and love between these warriors. This Truce involved the exchange of food and cigarettes, the singing of Christmas carols together, and even a friendly game of soccer. The idea of fierce enemies playing soccer, laughing, and celebrating together shows our true spirit shining through a situation that's contrary to our true nature. Any future attempts at such a holiday Truce in the years that followed were threatened with punitive actions by the officers.

I believe most people in most countries could be great friends regardless of their culture, and they don't have much time or energy to wish ill toward people in other countries.

Another true event is about one of our biggest American war heroes—Desmond T. Doss— who saved seventy-five men during World War II without ever firing his gun due to his Christian faith and dedication to "The Ten Commandments," one of which is "Thou Shall Not Kill." He joined the military and asked that he operate as a paramedic without a gun. He was initially humiliated, hazed, and tormented by his team in an attempt to force him to quit. Soldiers were dying at alarming rates, so to bring Desmond along without a gun was ludicrous to his superiors. To sum up the message he wanted to share (my interpretation), he was saying, "Thank you, General, for granting permission under war circumstances to kill people. However God says, 'Thou Shall not Kill,' and for that reason, I cannot carry a gun."

That is an interesting point, isn't it? There are things I

had never really pondered as I just accepted them as they were during circumstances of war. Nevertheless, we have all generally agreed that taking the life of another is the worst possible action we can take. But if one of our political leaders sends us out and says it's okay, it's somehow justified to kill people in large masses and even feel good about it.

Clearly, Desmond Doss saw the contradiction in this and wanted to be there to help salvage what he could. Despite the physical and mental abuse he endured, he didn't quit and not only served in World War II, but ran tirelessly through the night carrying wounded soldiers down Hacksaw Ridge on a rope to safety and care. It didn't take long for the soldiers and generals to become astounded at Desmond running around, as if he were invisible, saving men right under the enemy's nose, without them noticing. Instead of his platoon members laughing at him, they didn't want to go back in without him. This speaks volumes to me. This American hero even saved some Japanese "enemies" who were wounded, exemplifying the true meaning of forgiveness in that "We Are All One."

My fascination with our innate tendency to love one another should by no means be interpreted as undermining true heroes who voluntarily risk their lives to save innocent families and children from terrorism and other atrocities. Indeed, it's the self-sacrificing acts of our soldiers who fought for us and protected us that afford us the freedoms we enjoy today. Many soldiers have teared up describing events that took place during their time protecting civilians in an area of the world that was invaded and terrorized by the Taliban, Isis, or other ruthless groups. During these encounters, they describe local children they meet who, viewing them as heroes, race to them for hugs and candy bars.

To their horror, they simultaneously witness the most traumatic attacks on these innocent children and families right before their eyes. They explain on podcasts that these local people just want to live their lives with their families and go to work to serve and provide for their kids without being terrorized every day. These soldiers truly deserve recognition for their service and their willingness to protect the general welfare around the world, though it's unfortunate that it often comes at such a high cost, both physically and psychologically.

We may not be in a stage of enlightenment globally that would allow us to drop our guard and weapons today. But the next stage of enlightenment and gratitude to our heroes is to reciprocate their love and save lives by attracting and appointing world leaders who understand that the true wealth and welfare of any country is dependent on global humanitarianism and unity.

Historically, it has been our leaders that have conflicts, and the people in a country often have very little knowledge of the situation before some extreme act leads them into war. The media then often dehumanizes our opposition as a whole—not just the leaders who are the instigators. The entire population of a country is portrayed as uncivilized savages determined to hurt us. This often works because where there is fear, there's a lack of love.

During election time, we even see this "lack of love" encouraged among our various political factions. During an election cycle, there are unrelenting and inflammatory television commercials that encourage opposing political parties to accuse, judge, and argue. This keeps us too busy fighting one another to notice the lack of transparency and corruption that many believe exists all the way up the chain. Through fear and chaos, we leave ourselves vulnerable to manipulation, and we have no clarity about what's really happening around us and to us.

Many of the most shocking events in world history occurred when a leader was able to convince at least half the population to turn against the other half within the country, leading to civil war. If unity prevailed among the larger masses of people, the Hitlers of the world and other leaders of the same ilk couldn't get very far within their relatively small groups. Eckhart Tolle once said that we must take time to go within and scan our internal and external existence, or we may otherwise find unwanted visitors within our "house" (or body). If we apply this analogy to our state of mind when we make major decisions in choosing country leaders, we'll remain aligned and reflective versus angry and reactive. We will see through the toxic words of charismatic people who feed us lines we love to hear in order to receive our support. We will see that they don't have our best intentions at heart once they get into power.

Most countries currently have weapons of mass destruction, yet they want to control and block the other countries that have them. Who wants to be the only country without explosives? Nobody wants to drop their weapons when weapons are constantly pointed at them. We now have the technology to completely annihilate each other several times over. No one trusts anyone.

Still, I can't help but wonder what our world would be like if we all collectively chose leaders who were more "Christ-like, "Buddha-like," "Mohammed-like," or "God-like." The exact religious name—whether Muslim, Jewish, Christian, Buddhist, Hindu, or otherwise—doesn't distract me from the common message/values of love and truth that all of these religions stand for. Most of us identify with a certain religion, not by some widely accepted scientific finding or revelation, but because of the region we're from and the influence of our family. However, what we love about these amazing spiritual teachers emphasized in each religion is that they resemble what we envision as "God" or our highest self.

Desmond Doss, the man from World War I, was simply a man walking among us. He grew up with an abusive, alcoholic father, who was psychologically affected from serving in a war himself. Desmond, however, rose above his struggles, fears, and experiences of childhood violence, making a conscious choice to become "Christ-Like" (Christianity was his religion).

What if we all started this practice of following our light versus reliving the pain of our past? What if we spent our lives looking for ways to lift one another up, disallowing anyone to feel unloved or alone again? When it comes to attracting the ideal leaders we all so deeply desire, I think of Deepak Chopra's teaching about attracting the ideal companion: "Be the person you wish to have as a partner in life. If you would like to meet a romantic and thoughtful partner, then be a romantic and thoughtful partner." When you become what you're seeking, you recognize and attract this character in an individual. In essence, the world around you is a reflection of you. If you have ever felt chaos in your mind, you no doubt recognized that the world around you also felt chaotic, as it matched your state of mind at that time.

We have a saying for this truth: "When it rains, it pours." This is where decluttering our minds through meditation and grounding ourselves will allow logic, creativity, and answers to flow through us. Having leaders who foster logic, thoughtfulness, compassion, wisdom, interpersonal intelligence, integrity, ethics, and our true family values requires us to become these collective values in order to attract and recognize them in each other.

The Intellect of the Mind, Body, and Spirit

Currently, individuals with these qualities realize they can't lead most countries because anger and frustration can't coexist with love and logic. When I hear my patients complain about current political leaders, I think of the most loved, well-known individuals (whether they're living in physical form currently or not) and joke, "If only Mother Theresa or Oprah could have been president..." They laugh and say, 'Do you think that person would want the presidency position? They're too smart for that."

I recall my late grandpa once saying, "Why would anyone fight over the presidency? Look at President Obama. He went into the presidency looking like a baby and came out looking older than me! Instead of fighting over who gets to be president, they should be fighting over who gets to *not* be president!"

I value our freedom of speech and system of checks and balances. However, using these rights in a manner that's constructive and serves the intended purpose can get lost in the abuse of these rights to brew destruction, toxicity, and chaos. Being sharp-tongued and inflammatory doesn't equate to being more effective at problem-solving or conflict resolution. We haven't exactly packaged the position of the American presidency to truly attract the very best candidates.

I would like to reiterate that I have no political bias—I'm not endorsing any particular party or candidate. My intent is to write in the language of love, unity, and transparency, all of which cannot coexist with segregation, partisanship, demagoguery, and the kind of opposition that naturally exists with political affiliation.

Nor is this book intended to judge any individual, group, or process. I fully appreciate the experiences that had to happen exactly as they did in order for us to be here doing the very thing we're doing in this moment. Many of us have reflected considerably during this COVID-19 "pause" in our lives. We're standing up for one another, turning off autopilot mode, and contemplating our life purpose instead of defaulting to our old habits.

During the lockdown, we remained home and were able to see the blue skies again. We were able to breathe well through the break from excessive pollution in some of our most populated cities. We're fostering behaviors that create a more sustainable planet. Being less busy, we're currently experiencing fewer car accidents and enjoying the company of our families and loved ones who are finally home more often with us. We realize it's time to address relationships and expectations that no longer serve us well. Our leaders and experts are also reliant on each other to pull through a common cause together.

Now, to take bigger steps forward, can you imagine a day when our leaders can call each other for advice and gain from one another's strengths? What if a country whose economy has tanked for some time calls a more prosperous country like the U.S. for advice on what to thread into their system for improvement? They may not wish to fully change their system to become capitalist, but maybe they can come up with ideas to implement change with the advice of a leader who has been more successful at economics.

What if, in return, the U.S. acknowledged that the western diet and emphasis on productivity hasn't served our longevity or helped with our healthcare costs? Our leaders could reach out to a country that has the greatest longevity to weave in some ideas to help our people with our quality of life. We have people who are dying from hunger and people who are dying from eating far too much. What if we someday ascended to a point where we could replace the ex-penses on wars against each other with the far less costly expenses of finding our balance and expanding our humanity? Does this sound impossible?

Neale Donald Walsch's book *Conversations with God: Book 3* discussed how each individual state in the U.S. once operated completely independently, almost like their own little countries. When all states at that time discussed uniting to become the United States, many were hesitant that bordering states would fight and that it wouldn't work.

But how often do we see bordering states at war with each other in the U.S. these days? Despite all states having their own unique culture, different types of people, and different foods, we have learned not only how to coexist, but we also became one of the most powerful, free, and productive countries in the world through our union. This is not an all-or-nothing situation where we all completely abandon our practices in favor of one method.

However, some global harmony may allow us to see where we can collectively gain from and exchange with one another. Having some unity gives more power and alignment to dissipate corrupt forces. The existence of corrupt forces isn't just some other country's problem or just part of some people's culture to be tormented. With such corrupt beings dictating countries, it costs all of us an inconceivable amount by having to have our guards up for war, training, and most importantly, the cost of our beloved soldiers who end up having to defend us.

I'll circle back to Buddha's message that we create our world as the world is within us. When we work on fulfilling ourselves first (remember to put *your* oxygen mask on first) and allow the gratitude and abundance within to spill over onto your family, tribe, friends, coworkers, local strangers, and others across the world, you can create a new reality. This will spread like wildfire, and no doubt, we will eventually all be playing a friendly game of international soccer together and sharing fashion tips rather than sharing unjustified hate on the battlefields.

I love a particular quote from Buddha that describes how we can individually redefine ourselves and reinvent our world to reflect our highest self: "*We are what we think. All that we are arises with our thoughts. With our thoughts, we make the world.*" –Buddha

CHAPTER THIRTEEN

Our Children

Growing up, I had family and friends on both the Democratic and Republican "sides," so I heard both ends of the spectrum about how much energy and money should be spent on social welfare. I have seen the frustration of those who feel they're constantly paying for the "laziness" of others, who are allegedly not taking advantage of the same opportunities we all supposedly have equally. They feel we're enabling people to not try to become productive members of society. In some cases, this may hold some truth.

My husband and I are higher on the hierarchy of education and lucrative professions, so we end up being on the giving end of this spectrum versus the receiving end. However, I can't help but recognize a phenomenon that starts from birth into adulthood that allows me to see beneath the surface to pose the question to myself: are we all truly equal? To best entertain this question, let's discuss Abraham Maslow's Hierarchy of Needs, which he first developed in 1943.

Annahita Z. Van den Berghe

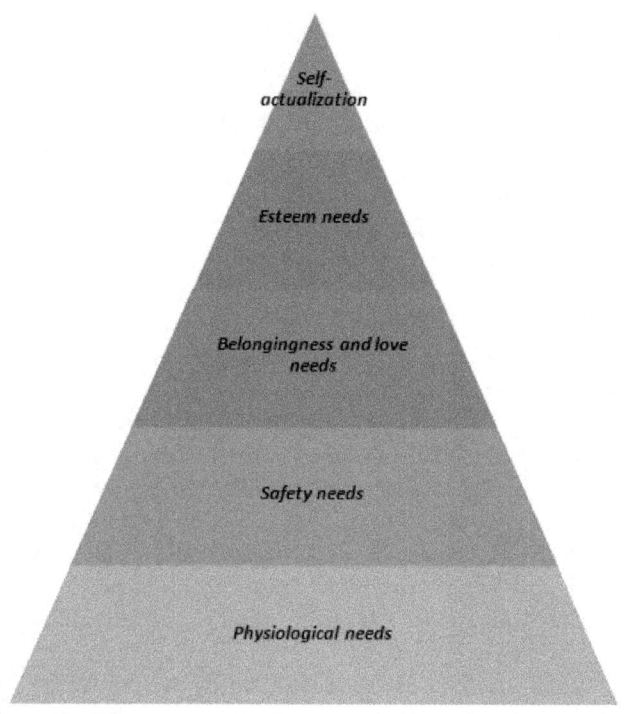

He created a pyramid (depicted above) describing the five stages people advance through in order to become the most valuable and contributing members of society that they can be:

Physiological needs at the bottom.

Safety needs next.

Belongingness and love needs next.

Esteem needs next, which refers to a feeling of accomplishment.

Self-actualization at the top or reaching our full

potential.

His theory was that we can't get to the top level until the needs on the lower levels are fulfilled. While there are some exceptions to this theory of human motivation, updates and revisions of Maslow's theory continue to support that when basic survival needs are not met, meeting your full potential becomes highly complicated.

But first, let's discuss the bottom level that symbolizes our basic human needs, which must be fulfilled before we can move through the other stages. These are our basic needs of food, water, nourishment, and sustainable temperatures, which we need just to exist. It's difficult to be productive in society when we're just trying to survive.

After our basic physiological needs comes Stage 2, which consists of our safety needs. A child needs to have parents or guardians who keep them protected and safe.

While many of us are blessed with parents who provide nourishment and safety, there are those who never had their basic and safety needs provided by a parent or guardian. It's valuable to note that this is independent of having significant wealth, resulting in a child's needs being better matched.

My parents came here from across seas in the early 1970s due to my father's outstanding scores in school, which differentiated us from the more common scenario of foreigners who are mainly able to come due to their extensive wealth. Despite this lack of wealth, our basic needs of food and safety, as well as the remainder of the pyramid stages were all amply met. And since I had highly educated family members, the thought of not going to college and making a large impact on society one day never would have occurred to me or to my brother. Our parents explained the ill effects of drugs and alcohol to us and were great role models, as they avoided all substances. We were also educated on the risks of sex and pregnancy. Our father was watchful to ensure my safety from strangers, and our parents rarely had us out of their sight or line of communication.

In contrast, addicted parents who are consumed in their own dramas may not be mentally sound to keep their kids safe from themselves or the people they attract into their lives.

I've spent a great deal of time with nurses who take care of children with special needs in their homes full-time. I know other physical therapists and physicians who work in hospital settings with children. It's surprising to hear about the parents of some of these kids who are in an unsound state of mind, starving their children despite being given government funds to help with groceries and other basic needs. The home nursing stories typically involved one parent (usually a single mom due to an absent father) who was on drugs and too engulfed in personal chaos, including abusive relationships, to even think twice about the fact that their young child was completely dependent on them for survival.

In instances where the abuse results in the death of a child, we then learn as a society what that child went through. Only it's too late by then. But wait, aren't there child welfare services that protect these children from all this bad stuff? Apparently, it's somewhat "hands off" from what I've heard from healthcare workers. As I write, the recent death of three-year-old Olivia Jansen has caused protests. People are upset that our child welfare system doesn't adequately protect kids like Olivia and others like Adrian Jones. In the latter, this young boy told authorities about the torture he was going through at home, but he wasn't taken seriously until after his death when the parents' personal video recording was found showing the heinous acts inflicted on him.

Let's suppose these two kids were never killed, but they were kept at a level of barely existing, which would be a more common scenario. We would have no concept of what they were enduring each day. Many of us would unwittingly judge these kids, wondering why they acted out in school. Later, as adults, people would judge them because they couldn't hold a job or perhaps act "normal." The question is: Is it realistic to have this expectation of people who never had the basics of food, safety, or love? Were we all truly given equal opportunities? While the opportunity is there for all to some extent, is it really that easy to get past these types of abuses? According to Maslow's theory, it would be highly unlikely without a village of compassion, love, and brain rewiring, not to mention a miracle.

Children growing up under such circumstances without their basic and safety needs met usually find it very difficult to move up the pyramid to the belonging and love stages where they're able to build healthy relationships and friendships. It's hard to engage in the trust and vulnerability of loving others.

I heard a great analogy to describe this phenomenon. Elephant keepers train baby elephants to not run away by chaining one of their legs to a post. The elephants struggle at first, but when they realize they're stuck, they stop trying to get away. Then, when they grow up, they still believe they're stuck, even though they've gotten big and strong enough to pull the post out of the ground and go free. Their minds are conditioned by their childhood experiences. The same is true for humans, which is why it's so challenging for those who didn't have their basic safety needs met to ascend to the fourth stage of "esteem" where they can become accomplished and build their presence in the world.

Some people may still say, "what does this have to do with me?" Well, we're all intertwined in direct or indirect, visible and invisible ways. The struggle or downward spiral of another has the potential to affect you, your family, your pocketbook, and your society. For starters, these deprived individuals are the ones in society that people complain about because they can't seem to hold a job or figure out contraception techniques, resulting in some people feeling they're punished for these irresponsible behaviors by having to pay for it in taxes. Some We consider this group as the bottom of society. They are the jobless, homeless, and poor.

Sometimes, people in this situation succeed in society from a monetary standpoint but never recover emotionally from their upbringing. In some cases, they might even reach a highly powerful role in society, all the while hiding their wounds or intentions of revenge behind a suit. These hurt and abused individuals prey on others through the abuse of their power. They're also the ones we see skimming millions of dollars off the top of organizations while contributing very little. Arguably, they cost more to our society than the ones at the bottom whom we accuse of soaking up funds.

These struggling kids who are fortunate enough to survive the hardships are more likely to become struggling adults with destructive behaviors to themselves and others. One of my patients, who is a lawyer, volunteers at local prisons. He studies prisoners and their behaviors, determining how to help them make better decisions to integrate into society. He told me that the number of prisoners who were abused and exploited as children has been found to be more than 99 percent! That's a staggering finding. Of course, I'm not implying that all abused individuals end up in prison, but the vast majority of prisoners report having been abused. They were never able to progress past the fight and struggle they endured just to exist, combined with a lack of love and security. That circumstance left them with an increased likelihood of criminal behavior. In this case, bridging the gap for these deprived individuals will create a safer and healthier environment for all of us.

Just as smiles and positive behaviors are contagious, toxic lifestyles and behaviors also spread within society. I have had several friends who grew up in highly accomplished families and fulfilled backgrounds, yet they still chose to build relationships with individuals who were abused and clearly exhibiting violent behavior. Many admit they've never recovered from the abuse and neglect they endured. The tender-hearted individual who walks right into the path of someone who is throwing punches from the unresolved pain of the past is accepting quite an undertaking. In one instance, I ran into a dear friend from high school who was wearing a pair of stylish sunglasses and looked great as usual. She had recently moved in with her boyfriend, and when I asked how things were going for them, she took off her sunglasses and privately showed me the bruises around her eyes. It was sickening to me because she's one of the most beautiful, confident, and intelligent people I know. It was surprising that she would accept this type of treatment, but it isn't an uncommon story. In this case, my friend was fortunate enough to leave the relationship and is happily married to another today. But I've known others who have experienced continued abuse and had children within these unstable relationships. This tends to perpetuate a vicious cycle and spread abuse down the family tree.

It may simply not be feasible for one person to replenish someone else's deficit of love and trust. It takes a village to bring healing, trust, and recovery before the group consciousness of love will prevail and allow healthy relationships and sound parenting to follow.

Many people feel that giving free services and goods to people who are in this situation is a waste of money and won't make any difference, as nothing given for free is appreciated. Others feel we aren't doing enough, and it's our duty to help one another. Is it possible that both are correct? I personally have yet to see an individual on welfare or other government support who didn't live well below the poverty line despite this support. Perhaps some funds are initially necessary to meet basic needs and to "stop the bleeding," so to speak. However, that may not be enough to restructure their belief system and the influences around them that prevent them from moving out of this cycle in order to meet their full potential. Remember that everyone is a genius at some type of intelligence, so they may simply need more help to find the love, passion, and purpose that await them. Children, in particular, can be impressionable and eager to soak up the care and advice of a mentor. This may not always be the case initially, but with enough time invested in them to demonstrate consistency, love, security, and good intentions, healthier seeds can be planted.

I had a patient who was a teacher until she stopped to start a large family of both biological and adopted children. As if adoption wasn't a big enough contribution, she started a foundation for kids who grew up in the inner city in dire circumstances. Their nourishment, safety, and security had all been violated. This foundation holds classes for the kids to teach them the skills required for job interviews, achieving scholarships, and thinking about their career, purpose, and service. This sounds more thorough to me. If you're going to hand a man a fish, you may as well teach him how to fish while you're at it.

Teachers are such valuable connection sources for children. They have a tremendous opportunity to touch lives and build character at the most pliable time in childhood. School systems are even starting to include meditation and yoga during classes. These are very powerful tools that I believe will serve the children during their entire lives. My father gave me these gifts when I was a child, and they brought me clarity, guidance, and an ability to attract everything that serves my highest purpose closer to me. They're more precious than any toy or dollar amount a child can receive.

When I was in physical therapy school, part of our curriculum included several visits to a school in an impoverished area close to the university. After classes, our PT class would go to this school and teach kids how to eat healthier and stay active, as well as how to prevent disease and injury. We would then practice our musculoskeletal assessments of range of motion, strength, and balance, and we would obtain their body mass index. At the end, we would play fun games such as "Freeze Tag" and "Red Rover," which I hadn't played since I was their age.

It was such fun to spend time with these kids who were pure potential for changing habits. They looked up to us in sincere gratitude, and their smiles and giggles were all the "thank yous" we needed.

While completing a fellowship in Applied Function Science, I learned that the instructor, Dr. Gary Gray was not only passionate about human movement/biomechanics, but he also had a family organization that holds camps and fundraisers for abused, neglected, and impoverished children. A part of our certification requirement for the forty-week fellowship was to serve as one of the coaches at a children's camp. We were told to expect 500 kids total, and each of us was assigned to four kids. I was quite nervous about losing one of my kids in this massive camp and because I simply didn't know what to expect. But I truly had the time of my life the minute I introduced myself to my four children, who were between the ages of three and six.

They had so much fun as they giggled about almost every activity we participated in. After four or five hours of camp activities and games, they devoured the pizza we provided as if it was the most phenomenal meal they'd ever had. Upon goodbye, all four of them tackled me with hugs. The little girl in the group made sure to look me square in the eyes and say, "I really like you." She had to come back for one more hug and picture together before she left with her mom. I teared up and said, "I love you, too, and I'm so proud of you!" She was the more open and verbal one out of my four, and I knew if she didn't approve of me and my services, she would have been sure to tell me!

Dr. Gray also supports an organization called "Not for Sale" that helps rescue exploited children both here in the U.S. and internationally. He shared his dream with us to have a commercial on the night of the Super Bowl to raise awareness about these exploited children. I learned at his event that the night of the Super Bowl has the largest occurrence of child trafficking.

Focusing on children creates our best odds for change in our current state and our future prosperity. This approach has been proven effective in world history. We're all aware of countries that were invaded and taken over through the slaying of men, enslaving of women, and brainwashing of the current and future children to conform to the ways of the new leader. A country or region in this situation often completely adopts the new way of life in terms of religion, culture, and life practices. If you give a knife to a surgeon, he will save lives. If you hand a knife to a murderer, he will take lives. This focus on raising compassionate, loving, fulfilled children can be the route to saving our future and the ascension of our spiritual realm.

Let's face it: not all of us are in a situation where adopting children or starting foundations is feasible, nor should we feel guilty about that. Fortunately, there are many easy steps we can take that collectively will make a bigger difference than the small percentage of individuals who are able to go above and beyond. We may simply start with sending our love, compassion, and non-judgment to children and focus our intentions, faith, and trust in what we would ideally like to see in our children collectively. Through blessing the situation, this step takes us away from judgment, blame, hopelessness, and loss of control. I once learned through a book called *Feelings Buried Alive Never Die* by Karol K. Truman that when we witness a situation that's contrary to our desires, it's great to bless since you can't bless something and judge it at the same time. Blessing a situation doesn't mean you agree with it and wish for more of it. It's simply a means of acceptance, coupled with the knowing that you can now consequently change its course to what's more aligned with you.

Most parents knowingly or unknowingly spend a great deal of time teaching their kids through example and words. When we reflect on what we've predominantly taught our kids, it's important to feel comfortable with the behaviors we've displayed in front of them. At times, our behavior contradicts what we say, so it's vital to continue setting our ideals high and teach our children why certain behaviors or outlooks are beneficial to them and others.

Even when parents have the great intention of ensuring their kids don't get taken advantage of in life, they can inadvertently teach competition, destruction, and animosity toward others.

They unwittingly pass on their own behaviors and insecurities that cultivate a mentality of lack. By this, I mean that if someone else succeeds or attains something, they believe it takes away from their operations. This creates separation and animosity between people.

This type of parenting emphasizes competition in everything from sports to grades to popularity. I see this aggressive approach occasionally when I help kids in therapy with sports performance. I often wish the parent would step back and allow their child to thrive without so much pressure on both of them. It doesn't mean parents shouldn't be present at games or rehab. But I believe they would see better sports performance, activity enjoyment, and even more harmony in their relationship with their child if they were more supportive than forceful.

I was once in the midst of a treatment session with a well-known professional athlete when the mother of a young patient walked over to him and said, "We are very big fans of yours. Do you do any side training? My son is getting therapy here. He has all the talent and could go so far if he only applied himself more. We try to push him, but he needs work on getting less distracted. I know he would do it for you if you trained him."

My patient shook his head and said with a smirk, "I can't teach your kid to have passion for something he doesn't. You either really want it, or you don't. Passion and drive aren't skillsets to be taught." The mother looked surprised at his candid response and walked away embarrassed.

In contrast to teaching a mentality of fear and lack, we have the option to raise our children to envision abundance as limitless. Their potential is limitless, so we can remind them that there is no real competition for any of us. Every single one of us is literally irreplaceable. Most importantly, we need to remind ourselves that life is supposed to be as playful as children innately are. Teaching our kids how to be grateful, appreciative, and generous will bring more abundance and success into their lives in every respect from finances to the types of companions they attract as spouses, friends, and business partners.

The next easy, yet most powerful step we can take is to teach our kids sensitivity and compassion toward one another. Parents report much damage from bullying and cyber bullying these days, but let's consider the flipside. Our children have the potential to have an equally powerful positive influence on each other's lives. If we teach them to do so, they can lift, love, and inspire.

I once learned from Qigong masters Justin and Sharon Orth that "kids are really smart . . . until we dumb them down." They naturally know they're limitless . . . until we teach them limits. My freshman year at KU, I listened to a lecture on the topic of love in contrast to racism and separation. The speaker was famous rap artist and actor Ice-T. He said, "If you put five young kids of all ethnicities—white, Hispanic, black, etc.—in a large playground sandbox and give them a bunch of toys to play with, they will all start playing together and have a great time building and creating together. Not one of them will so much as notice that each child is of a different color or ethnicity, nor will they judge that person based off of it. They will not separate and segregate based off class or denominations. All that they want is to connect, play, and create with one another." What a powerful observation that has stayed with me for more than twenty years now.

As a parent, the best we can ask for is to create a solid foundation from our best selves and pass the torch to our kids, hoping they'll take our teachings to the next level. I love this quote by author and speaker Esther Hicks: "Children coming forth today have a greater capacity to deal with the greater variety of information that is coming forward than you did. They deliberately are coming forth into this environment where there is more to contemplate. This generation gap that you are talking about has ever been thus. Each new generation, every new individual, that comes forth, is coming with you having prepared a different platform for them to proceed from. There is this thing that gets in the way of that that says, 'I'm the parent. I got here first. I know more than you do.' From the children's perspective, and from the purity of their Nonphysical Perspective, what they are saying is 'You're the parent. You got here first. You prepared a platform that I am leaping off from, and my leap will be beyond anything that you have ever known.'" (Excerpted from a speech given in San Rafael, California on February 27, 1999.)

The pivotal point to our collective physical, mental, and spiritual expansion is in our ability to teach our kids every valuable pearl we know during the short time we have with them. In this way, we pass the baton to them with the sincere hope that they will run faster, jump higher, and fly to unimaginable heights.

Despite enduring an unsound childhood and not having their basic and safety needs met, there are still many superheroes in this world who came out of their childhood passionate about helping others avoid the same fate or survive it. They made a conscious decision to become the opposite of their parent/s.

Abusers don't live forever, of course, and it's an

impactful moment when someone who was abused realizes they have the power to bury the abuse along with the abuser. By choosing not to pass the abuse down the family tree, survivors can put the horrific story to rest.

We've all had our share of events that I lovingly refer to as "life's curveballs." Regardless of the origin of the event, the principle of "love is always the answer" applies. There's a deeper message and always an opportunity to better the cause. In most cases, people come out of these situations saying, "God wouldn't give me more than I can handle" with a knowing that they will conquer that hill.

As I mentioned earlier, I endured a very complicated pregnancy that left us in the NICU experiencing a daily rollercoaster ride for so long a time that many in the hospital came to believe I worked there. As each neighbor of our pod in NICU came and left, graduating to their homes, my son and I remained, not knowing if both of us would ever leave the hospital alive. At one point, we went through so many traumatizing events in such a close timeframe that a hospital psychologist asked if my husband and I needed emotional support. I thanked her and told her that considering the circumstances, we were weathering the storm quite well and had chosen to remain hopeful no matter what presented day to day. We chatted a bit about how we would support our son in any direction he chose to go. "After all, he's in the driver's seat," I told her. "Whatever direction he chooses, we trust that that outcome will be good."

The psychologist said she was pleasantly surprised at how we were handling everything and asked me how we managed to stay so positive considering our painful circumstances. I told her that in our household, we practice meditation and positive affirmations. We focused on loving our son in the hospital just as we would if he were at home. We visualized him home and even had a blown-up picture of him next to our bed as if he were there with us. The psychologist responded, "It sounds like you two are handling all this in the healthiest way possible. You know, I try and tell my clients about meditation and energy work. I tell them that I know it doesn't sound tangible in the midst of a crisis, but somehow, it simply works for individuals who use it. I wish more parents here at the NICU would try these alternative methods." She then offered me her card in case I wanted to reach out to her later.

It would be insincere to tell you that I never felt overwhelmed or fearful. However, I made a commitment to my son, and I knew that entailed my ability to let go of the fears, concerns, and bleak projections of even the biggest experts. I didn't want anything to remove my clarity from making sound decisions in this life-altering circumstance. I knew I had to remain omnipresent, not lost in the perceived fears of the future. I turned my fears to gratitude for what we had overcome despite the struggles.

I appreciate the gifts of having been in that situation in the hospital for so long. I knew it was no accident, and the purpose was there whether I could understand it fully at the time or not. For starters, I knew the ropes there and knew them well. I knew all the valuable resources the hospital had to support my son. He had cycled through just about every doctor in the system, and I knew all the best ones to turn to. I had gained a new skill and ability that I never knew I had—how to survive extended life in the NICU!

I knew so much by then that I helped countless other moms in the NICU who came and left as our neighbors there. I listened to their fears and worries, most of which were hurdles I'd already surpassed months before. I was able to offer my insight on most topics, having been through them. We created bonds and shared prayers over our children. I rejoiced with them when they graduated from the hospital and used their success as ammunition that someday, we, too, would leave the hospital. We just had to. Once the storm blew over—and eventually, it always will—I wouldn't have changed anything that occurred despite the fact that they were the most trying times of my life. My husband and I never thought we could learn so much from a little being who weighed in at a whopping two and a half pounds at one point.

There's a quote in *Conversations with God* that really spoke to me and helped me move toward non-judgment of past traumatic occurrences in my life. To paraphrase it, contrast exists because it highlights what we truly desire and stand for. We would have no concept of anything meaningful if its contrast didn't exist. In other words, how would we know light if there was no darkness? With this perception, we can let go of any resentment toward anyone or any experiences as they only helped form who we are and what we truly value in life. Eventually, we can learn to experience the positive without the need for contrast. We can also appreciate that contrast exists in this world and choose to go within, where we can be guided by our internal compass. This can feel more like riding the waves versus swimming upstream.

Once we release judgment about any events in our past that felt like contrast, we can, in essence, transform or recreate the past experiences that we always wished we had. If you lacked love and security growing up, you can be loving and protective to yourself, your kids, your pets, and others. You can be supportive and present about their activities and interests. You can prioritize family and choose a partner who comes from a place of love and light to further instill family values and traditions that you feel you missed out on.

Our kids are a direct reflection of us. The love and happy experiences we provide them will also circulate happiness back to us. We, too, are the child, the parent, and All That Is.

CHAPTER FOURTEEN

The Life Cycle

It's easy to fear what we know little about. Some of us are on a quest to find immortality through some form of age reversal behavior that we've termed a "midlife crisis." We fear that pain and suffering are an inevitable part of death, and some even hold beliefs about eternal pain and suffering depending on our deeds in life. However, pain and suffering are not a part of the experience of "death" so much as a potential experience during life. The "cause" of death is just a moment in time. Everyone leaves life in some exiting vehicle, and the mode of "transportation" isn't as significant as the love we shared with that person during life and how they impacted us.

I was blessed to listen to Chopra Center cofounder David Simon's last speech before he passed away in physical form. Ironically, he was a neurologist who diagnosed his own brain tumor. During his lecture, he told us his story about how he diagnosed his cancer while he was attempting to parallel park and noticed he had a blind spot. This prompted him to perform a neurological examination on himself.

Halfway through his lecture, he experienced a malfunction due to the brain tumor and told us the story from the beginning all over again. It was a very touching and humbling lecture that I'll never forget. He looked very peaceful up there, and I could easily sense the love of the Chopra team for him.

To my surprise, an audience participant asked him, "How are we supposed to have faith in all of these teachings when we see you dying of a brain tumor?" It was a very candid question, and I felt uncomfortable with it since it was clear David had reached his last days. Nevertheless, he smiled and replied, "God has a sense of humor."

I took his statement to mean that God's perception of death may be far different from ours. Deepak Chopra's analogy on the topic is intriguing. He says that death is perhaps like waking up from a dream and realizing, "Oh, wow, that was just a dream! Nothing to worry about. It wasn't even real." Maybe we wake up after death and realize, "Oh, wow, that was just life! Nothing to worry about here."

Of course, I'm not implying that what we do in life has no meaning, but we may have a drastically different perception of life once we graduate from our physical existence. Many spiritual teachers suggest that there's no such thing as death because our soul is eternal. We have a physical vehicle that we use to navigate life which is nothing more than an honorable uniform, so to speak. Deepak Chopra once wrote that in effect, if we're talking on the phone, and suddenly our call is dropped, neither party suddenly fails to exist. Our line of communication has merely been disrupted.

Language is something we have made up as our main form of communication in our respective countries, though I believe our soul speaks the universal language of silence. It's an understanding through an exchange of energy and intention. It may be communication through intuition. Many people who "lost" someone they held dear in life report feeling their presence after they've left the physical. Some even "check in" with their departed loved one when making decisions and feel they get a response or direction. Some receive what they believe are communications in a dream.

It isn't necessary to experience "death" to have this type of connection and communication without words with one another, however. Have you ever thought of someone you hadn't spoken to in months or even years, only to have them call at random at that very moment? Identical twins often have these types of experiences of intuitively knowing what the other is feeling or experiencing without being in physical proximity of each other at the time. We tend to tap into these abilities more when our loved ones leave their physical form because we no longer have verbal language to fall back on. It's very similar to how we learn a new language best when we visit the country and are forced to only use that new language until it becomes second nature. Our physical language and traditional means of communication can become a barrier in developing more of our metaphysical capabilities.

Of course, we still miss our loved ones when they leave us in physical form. Often, they're more prepared for their departure than those of us still living and wishing to hold on to them longer. It's a very natural feeling to miss the experiences and adventures you had with that beloved individual. I view our life on Earth as a wondrous gift of an all-inclusive, limitless, and timeless vacation with our loved ones. We know that no matter how much fun we're having on our time away, toward the end of any vacation, we always look forward to the comfort and peace of returning home. However, we don't need to obsess over our return from the beginning or the midpoint of our valued vacation. We merely need to value our time here and enjoy every experience that allows our highest expression with the awe of a child. When on vacation, we enjoy the new perspectives of the locals and the culture. We eat well and recharge until our last night when it's time to prepare for our return home. The intention of this material is to help us live life more fully during whatever length of time serves our highest purpose on this joint venture. We can make a difference in any length of time that we exist. It all has purpose and meaning in fully realizing who we are.

Oprah Winfrey had a baby at the age of fourteen, who lived for only two weeks. She only recently named her son and realized far later in life that his birth was a pivotal point in her taking control of her life, ending the abuse she was enduring and making a shift from victimization to empowerment. That's quite a purpose and catalyst for a little boy with a lifespan of merely two weeks.

When I compare life to a vacation, I'm not implying that we reduce the purpose of living to lying around, drinking, and doing nothing of value. When Leonardo da Vinci created the Mona Lisa over a span of twenty years, I imagine it wasn't easy. When Michelangelo painted the Sistine Chapel, some were sure he would fall on his face due to its complexity. It took four years of hard work to create that masterpiece. However, I'll bet both of these artists had the time of their life creating their work despite the effort and energy.

This is my wish for us. We create our grandest legacy that we can look at with awe and have a blast while we're at it. When it's then time to "return home," we pile on the party bus, realizing that each one of us has our own unique stop for returning Home. We're grateful for the unforgettable time together with a focus on what each individual's life purpose offered this world versus the focus of their moment of departure.

This mind, body, and spirit concept has humbled some of our greatest minds, yet curiosity and wonder are what bring the utmost exhilaration, knowing that our storyline unfolds throughout this lifelong journey. As complex as it all appears, it's the simple things in life that bring us to those moments of truth and understanding.

In walking this path, I've fallen thousands of times and will probably fall a thousand times more. With the determination of a child learning how to walk for the first time, no matter how many times I tumble, trip, or topple, I will rise again. I will gleam with confidence that I will walk effortlessly with purpose and grace by virtue of the journey.

This very morning, my daughter ran to me with a big smile, holding out a beautiful fuchsia-colored flower that she picked for me. I reflected on the innate wisdom of our children to remain in the moment and simply be happy just for the sake of spreading that happiness. This gift of my daughter's flower is highly symbolic. I realized that the day I denounce my yearning for truth, love, growth, and understanding is the day my expansion ends and the beautiful petals of my life begin to wilt.

Some of my favorite spiritual teachings are the beautiful lines from our most famous Persian poet, whom we all know and love—Rumi. There is so much truth and perspective to allow self-healing, understanding of experiences, and wisdom dating back to the mid-1200s.

Here are some of my favorite Rumi teachings that I was immersed in while growing up in the Persian culture that has been home to some of the most beautiful and resonating poetry and poets of all time.

1. There is a saying in Farsi that paraphrases Rumi's quotes/teachings on the law of attraction. It reads, "Del beh del Rah dareh," which translates in English to there is a direct path created from your heart to the heart of those and that which you love. What you are fond of is also fond of you and has a direct path toward you the moment you feel or create that love or special interest.

2. There is a teaching to be mindful of the company you seek. Rumi teaches to stay close to the experiences and people who allow the life force within you to emanate versus those that take you toward disease or regression in mind, body, and spirit.

3. Rumi exemplifies how to be in a state of "drunkenness" from the same love source that resides within all of us. This state of happiness is not conditional, as it must be maintained despite wounds or hardships of the past. Our inner light shines the brightest through those wounds or in comparison to that darkness we may experience in life.

These poems and his quotes can be found on *everydaypower.com*. I highly recommend that you immerse yourself in this wisdom.

My wish to you, to us, and to humanity is complete health of mind, body, and spirit. No one aspect can thrive independently.

Below is a list to help you sum up what I believe are key aspects to our inner and outer glow, inner and outer beauty, longevity, unity, world peace, and enlightened path to our self-created heaven enjoyed right here, right now on planet Earth.

1. Start with yourself to initiate a healthy dose of self-love and kindness every day.

2. Eat Divinely. High quality, unprocessed, organic, humanely raised foods. (Keep your fridge full, not your pantry.)

3. Eat majority plant-based with animal products more sparingly in comparison to your ample fruit, vegetable, and legumes intake.

4. Get plenty of sleep and rest. Shoot for at least seven to eight hours of quality sleep nightly.

5. Unplug and be present.

6. Surround yourself with nature.

7. Spend more time with yourself in silence than in crowds or on social media.

8. Exercise like an endurance athlete. Slow and steady wins the race!

9. Practice moderation in everything you do.

10. Be mindful of how your body and mind feel, and adjust your activities accordingly.

11. Take well-calculated risks once in a while to fully realize your passion and potential.

12. Embrace your family, friends, community, country, and planet.

13. Love all creatures of life with a special place for children and animals. They reflect the innocence and child in you!
14. Do not partake in self-pity. Embrace your power!
15. Be the change you wish to see in the world.
16. Be an angel in someone's life, even if they're a complete "stranger."
17. Love is always the answer.

Eat Well, Rest Fully, Love Passionately, Love Expansively, Dream Big, Believe with all your Heart, and Know Your Path to Your True Self is Within.

My favorite Rumi quote that I'll leave you with is: "Out beyond ideas of wrongdoing and right doing there is a field. I'll meet you there."

References

GIFT Fellowship Training
2019 (40-week training live and interactive webinars): One my most impactful learning experiences
Dr. Gary Gray, Dr. Dave Tibiero, Doug Gray, AFS

International Pain and Spine Institute lectures:
One of my most impactful University instructors and mentors: Adrian Louw, PT, Ph.D.

THE GUT-BRAIN CONNECTION: FACTS, FADS & FALLACIES (Live Interactive Webinar) 6/30/2020
Dr. Gina Willett (Ph.D., R.D.)

Journey into Healing
2/27/2016-3/01/2016
Dr. Deepak Chopra, M.D.
Dr Andrew Weil, M.D.
Dr. Tieraona Low Dog, M.D.
Dr. Suhas Kshirsagar, M.D.

Journey into Healing
10/2011
Dr. Deepak Chopra, M.D.
Dr. Valencia Porter, M.D.
Dr. David, Simon, M.D.

Mindfulness and Stress Reduction: A workshop for Healthcare Professionals
7/17/2020
Professor Kent Howard, M.A. MBSR certified

Inspirational Readings:
The Blue Zone Solution by Dan Buettner

The Intellect of the Mind, Body, and Spirit

The Book of Secrets: Unlocking the Hidden Dimensions of your Life by Deepak Chopra, M.D.

Quantum Healing by Deepak Chopra, M.D.

The Spontaneous Fulfillment of Desire: Harnessing the Infinite Power of Coincidence by Deepak Chopra, M.D.

Super Brain by Deepak Chopra, M.D. and Rudolph E. Tanzi, Ph.D.

Conversations with God series by Neil Donald Walsch

Diet for a New America by John Robbins

Harmonic Wealth by James Arthur Ray

What I Know For Sure by Oprah Winfrey

Documentaries

What the Health written, produced, and directed by Kip Andersen and Keegan Kuhn

The Game Changers directed by Louie Psihoyos, produced by Joseph Pace and James Wilks, written by Mark Monroe and Joseph Pace

Acknowledgments

A sincere thank you to Melanie Votaw, my brilliant editor who uses her unique genius to help authors like myself to have a voice in this world.

My gratitude to my inspirational patients who taught me how to have trust, humility, and the indomitable spirit to change the fabric of reality under any circumstance. You've enlightened me more than you know, and for this, I'm forever grateful.

A special thank you to physicians like Dr. Khadavi and other healthcare providers whose brilliance and dedication to taking healthcare to a different level is the very catalyst that will make that vision a reality for all of us.

Thank you to all my instructors and mentors throughout my journey. A special thank you to Gary Gray who impacted my physical therapy journey since I was a student. It's easy to tell other people how to be a "better" person. It is another level of character and truth when you live by example. You've set the bar high in mind, body, and spirit, and we will aim high to reach that standard and pay it forward, thanks to you.

Thank you to my father and mother who lead by example in how to have compassion, forgiveness, and a trust in something bigger than ourselves. You are always present to guide us. You persistently and patiently planted the seeds despite the time it took for that enlightenment to flourish within us.

They say the people you must run to keep up with will be the people who will advance you the furthest in life.

My dear brother, you have kept me running to catch up to your discoveries since we were very little. I'll always look up to you in sincere gratitude for your love, support, and laughs through thick and thin. Your beautiful heart and beautiful family have enriched my life more than you know.

Thank you to my children and four dogs who remind me every day to live in laughter and spontaneity, to dismiss struggles and grudges, exude unconditional love, embrace the moment, and enjoy all the fun under any circumstances.

Last, but certainly not least, thank you to my husband, who always encouraged me to share my genius with the world. When lost in life struggles and circumstances, you tirelessly and relentlessly remind me of my gifts and talents, as well as who I really am.

ABOUT THE AUTHOR

Dr. Annahita Z. Van den Berghe (Anna) graduated from the first class of the Doctor of Physical Therapy program in the region at Rockhurst University and holds an Exercise Science degree from Kansas University. She completed a forty-week fellowship in Biomechanics and Applied Functional Science through the world-renowned Gray Institute in 2019.

With a passion for total health in mind, body, and spirit, Anna added to her general continuing education physical therapy courses by taking medical seminars on diet, well-being, meditation, energy healing, and Ayurvedic (the science of life) principles. She has treated patients ranging from professional athletes to senior citizens and has been a successful director for one of the country's largest physical therapy corporations.

Passionate about spreading health and wellness within the community, Anna held bootcamp and dance classes for healthcare providers at her physical therapy clinic. She is dedicated to lifelong learning, so she's currently taking a year-long Total Health teachers course with the Deepak Chopra Center's most prominent physicians. She will receive three new certifications in diet, meditation, and life coaching in 2021.

www.ingramcontent.com/pod-product-compliance
Lightning Source LLC
LaVergne TN
LVHW020929090426
835512LV00020B/3284